Young British Archite

Jeremy Melvin

Young British Architects

Birkhäuser
Basel · Berlin · Boston

A CIP catalogue record for this book is available from the Library of Congress, Washington D.C., USA

Deutsche Bibliothek Cataloging-in-Publication Data

Young British architects / Jeremy Melvin. - Basel ; Berlin ; Boston : Birkhäuser, 2000

ISBN 3-7643-6153-0
ISBN 0-8176-6153-0

© 2000 Birkhäuser Verlag, P.O.Box 133, CH-4010 Basel, Switzerland

Printed on acid-free paper produced from chlorine-free pulp

Layout and cover design: Martin Schack, Dortmund

Printed in Germany

ISBN 3-7643-6153-0
ISBN 0-8176-6153-0

987654321

Contents

Footsteps into the Next Century – Preparations for an Architectural Renaissance

One evening in July 1997, two months after an Electoral landslide swept him to power, Tony Blair hosted a reception at his official residence, 10 Downing Street, for members of the 'design community'. For several years the Labour Party, perhaps striving for the aura of Francois Mitterrand's *Grand Projets*, had struggled to devise a cultural policy which embraced architecture; a report by Demos, a Centre-Left think tank, which argued that 'creative industries' made a significant contribution to the entire British economy, became one of New Labour's intellectual cornerstones. The way opened for architecture to become a legitimate part of the political process, and it became harder to take the view which British policy makers had long cherished, that architecture is an unnecessary luxury. For the first time in decades, architects smelt a whiff of power, and in a gesture which fitted the host's affinity for youth, guests included some of those featured in this book. Blair likes to call his party New Labour to denote its break with the past. His guestlist suggested that he wanted to associate his political newness with novelty in architecture.

That warm summer evening leant a superficial glamour to a complicated process which had started much earlier. Several factors had already begun to change the position of architecture within the political spectrum, and even before the General Election, they had started to interweave, although without conscious co-ordination. Few owed a direct debt to Labour policies. Design standards had already begun to rise under the previous, Conservative, government led by John Major. The government itself started to set a better example in its own buildings though often only after a public relations disaster. An example is the Inland Revenue Centre (i.e. tax collecting) in Nottingham. The original design provoked such an outcry that it was scrapped, and a design competition held to replace it, which was won by Michael Hopkins and Partners. Even more important were the design quality quidelines which specified that most projects receiving a grant from the highly successful National Lottery had to show design quality.

Changes in the way public funds were allocated for building also created opportunities. These were especially beneficial to imaginative proposals for urban regeneration or combinations of activities such as health, leisure and education. Coincidentally, new trends in lifestyle led to a demand for more urban homes, bars and shops in metropolitan centres like London and Manchester. At the same time, a slow and uncertain recovery began from the recession of the early 1990s, which had devastated architectural practices, delayed chances to build for many of the architects in this book, and fundamentally altered the conditions in which architects work.

When this upturn came, it was obvious that its architecture would bear almost no resemblance to buildings of the previous boom of the late 1980s, which was almost entirely a private sector phenomenon. The 1990s are different both in function, having seen many buildings for cultural purposes, and in architectural idiom. The sources of this idiom, or idioms because there is no single, homogenous 'style', come from a series of powerful formative influences which architects in this book share. All qualified during the 18 years of Conservative government between 1979 and 1997; few had built very much before the recession spread its icy grip from 1990 onwards. Part-time teaching became a vital source of income for many young architects, so the influence of architectural schools remained stronger for this generation than others who became more quickly involved with the demands of practice.

Most schools of architecture during this period grappled with the legacy of modernism. This legacy may be universal to architecture schools in the western world, but in Britain it had a particular flavour. One of the by-products of the consensus which emerged in Britain after 1945 was the adoption of modernism as the architectural idiom for the new schools, universities, hospitals and housing which characterised the social policies of the time. Long after the simplistic manifesto-like claims of modernist pioneers had been rejected in architectural circles, their effects remained a strong latent influence as they had penetrated so far into society. Thatcher's election in 1979 confirmed that the consensus was over; the political policies which had allowed that penetration would no longer be pursued. The state ceased to be a major client for buildings, a factor which had underpinned earlier generations of architects and ensured plenty of employment opportunities. Without the support of its ideological programme, modernism became a pragmatic, enabling series of formal devices and tactics, equally applicable to many contexts and for many functions. And, without the moral umbilical cord which tied modernist architecture to social progress, modernism had to justify its existence alongside various traditionalist approaches which took hold in the early 1980s. A great variety of approaches to architecture arose, which by coincidence neatly suited the economic conditions and political aims which emerged in the 1990s. This flexibility also, perhaps, opened the way for modern architecture to engage, for the first time in Britain, in a meaningful dialogue with existing urban fabric, just as it made the relationship between architecture and politics problematic.

These transformations to modernism paved the way for the embrace which the Labour Party offered to architecture in 1997; post-modernism, which held sway in the commercial boom of the late 1980s and which in Britain was an almost entirely blind alley, could never have had more than a token presence in a political programme, even if the free-market policies pursued under Margaret Thatcher's premiership had found space for architecture at all. The emerging architecture of the 1990s, by contrast, with its slick aesthetic appeal, and because the traces of a social programme were relegated to style rather than adopted in substance, it was a perfect visual analogue to New Labour politics. Political recognition confirmed the acceptance of such trends into the mainstream, and the apparent affinities between design, popular culture, and a new political settlement led the American magazine *Newsweek* to brand London as the coolest city on the planet.

Politics and popular culture seemed to be moving in tandem. This is a heady combination for architecture, which needs political will and thrives on popular recognition. But its glamour can be superficial. Architectural trends and even individual projects often work to timescales which are profoundly unpolitical. The architects represented in this book may have some important common factors in their backgrounds, and have achieved some prominence and received opportunities under a Labour government whose aims some, at least, might share, but they are also addressing issues which architects will face for several decades, whatever political programmes are pursued. Having demonstrated a degree of engagement with these issues is a primary criterion for selecting those firms in this book. It does not try to cover all aspects of work by young architects in Britain; nor are the architects here necessarily the 'best' which would be either a meaningless subjective judgement or depend on self-referential norms about 'good architecture'.

There are also many talented architects of this generation who are rising to senior positions in established offices, and several independent practices who, at the time of selection, may have designed some consummate projects which elegantly deal with empirical, contingent factors, but of insufficient range or depth to indicate what they might add to theoretical and conceptual architectural concerns. Engaging with the discipline of architecture at a deeper level than the particularities of single projects is a characteristic of all those selected.

Some of these concerns are relatively simple and obvious. Among them are an ability to respond to new ways of working which changes in the client base require. Architects now have to be entrepreneurial, not just as good business managers, but in demonstrating the advantages of building projects to clients who might not even have decided to invest in construction – a reversal of one of the most persistent myths in recent British architectural lore, which has Norman Foster announcing to clients that they didn't need a new building, but a new management structure.

Other concerns are vaguer, but no less pressing, such as an ability to find creative and innovative ways of addressing transport problems, i.e. road congestion and inadequate public transport, or understanding what a new work of architecture might contribute to a particular context, especially in run-down inner cities. Yet more affect the evolution of architecture as a discipline, how the traditional typologies of form and function might develop, or how art and architecture are related, given that neither stands still. But underlying all these important matters is one common theme: how architecture, the discipline which manipulates form, space, energy and surface can mediate between given environments and the aspirations of people and organisations who use them. Britain has a surfeit of rundown inner cities, a shortage of open land and almost no wilderness; it is also undergoing dramatic political reform. In these conditions architecture is not just the product of political circumstance. It is also a strategy for projecting the future. To show how this might transpire is one aim of this book.

It is tempting to place an emerging generation in the categories which applied to their predecessors, to trace lines of development. They certainly exist: FAT (Fashion Architecture Taste) engage with some of the themes which provoked NATO in the early 1980s (Narrative Architecture Today, an informal group which formed at the AA, with Nigel Coates as probably its best known figure. Its concerns were wit, fun and enjoyment, and one might regard them as a distant and not very serious descendant of the Situationalists). Foreign Office Architecture owe some debt to OMA; the interest in the 'ordinary' which motivated Peter and Alison Smithson and the Independent Group in the 1950s re-emerges in projects as different as those of FAT and Caruso St John. And the Classicists, who grouped themselves around the Prince of Wales in the mid-1980s, have had very little influence on those who were students or young architects at the time, and their attempts to create a school of architecture at the Prince of Wales' Institute of Architecture have ended in failure.

Such connections are only superficial guides to the ideas and influences behind architecture. Searching for them alone overstresses similarities and underestimates influences from outside architecture, as well as several extremely important changes in education and practice between these generations.

The following section outlines these developments, as a background to understanding the projects illustrated in this book.

From the 1970s onwards, architectural education had to face up to the legacy of modernism. Some schools evolved a more creative approach to it than others, and they were not always the most famous. Liverpool University, weighed down with its own heritage as the oldest university school of architecture in the country, and the internecine political warfare and economic decline of its city, was no longer the force it had been when it educated Colin Rowe, Robert Maxwell and James Stirling in the 1940s. The Architectural Association in London lost its public subsidy and paying the full cost of fees made it an unattractive or impossible proposition for British students who could study at other schools for nothing; unlike earlier generations of British architects, graduates of these two schools do not dominate, although the AA remained an international beacon and still set a pace which other schools tried to follow. Meanwhile Cambridge University evolved a particular view of architecture with Dalibor Vesely as its leading intellectual light and Eric Parry as its most notable practitioner today; drawing on phenomenology it moved away from the quantitative analytical techniques which it had pursued under the leadership of Sir Leslie Martin. Bath, the only university of those founded in the 1960s to have an architecture school, promoted an approach which verred between formalism and pragmatism, which owed much to the synthesis of form and technology found in the work of Arup Associates, and the engineering philosophy of Ted Happold, one of its first professors.

Particularly influential was the school at Kingston, an affluent south western suburb of London, and especially the teaching duo of David Dunster and Jon Corpe. They addressed the modernist legacy directly. Whatever the claims and achievements of its pioneers, it represented a formal language which could engage with any programme or context. Dunster, the intellectual of the two, theorised this approach through a sophisticated reading of Italian Rationalism, which greatly expanded the scope for modernism to engage with physical context and cultural ideas, and through American post modern theory, which offered new readings of the relationship between architecture and society. Students from the school began to move into many of the leading architectural firms, especially Stirling Wilford, Ahrends Burton and Koralek and Terry Farrell and Partners, all of which had already started to expand beyond the traditional modernist agenda. They included Richard Portchmouth and Mike Russum of Birds Portchmouth Russum, and, after Dunster and Corpe moved to the Bartlett School of University College London, all the partners of Allford Hall Monaghan Morris and Farshid Moussavi of Foreign Office Architects. Dunster has since become professor of architecture at Liverpool University.

The greatest new influence in education, however, came from a change in administration rather than the work of particular teachers. Architectural education in Britain is split into three parts, each of which has to be passed before candidates have the legal right to call themselves architects. The first two parts are academic qualifications, typically the first being awarded after three years' study and the second after a further two. The third part requires at least two years practical experience. Until the mid-1980s, schools of architecture expected that students would stay with them for five years and made very little attempt to weed out those who were not suitable for the course;

now students have to re-apply for the post-graduate course and many take the opportunity to apply to different schools. Students now tend to sample a much wider range of educational approaches and, strengthened by exchange programmes between European universities, British schools have become far more outward-looking than they were 20 years ago. Many of the architects in this book benefited from this more open climate; some helped to instigate it.

Greater openness and flexibility also came from relationships with architectural magazines. Britain is unusual in having as many as two weekly and three monthly magazines devoted to architecture, most of which are read by most architects. There are also numerous other publications, both aimed at business and consumer readerships, which cover architecture, and national newspapers and broadcasters often mention it. The level of discussion may fail to excite specialists, but it does exist. The generation of architects represented in this book had opportunities for publicity, even when recession severely limited opportunities to build.

Recession also prodded them to be more flexible and less ideological about the type and size of commissions they would be prepared to take, a process encouraged by changes in the way public funds were distributed as the recession receded. One of these developments was the Single Regeneration Budget. It amalgamated government funds which had previously been distributed between various ministries, such as transport, education, health and the environment, who followed rigid policies in distributing them. As a consequence, architectural solutions tended to be extrapolations of government rules. Once a need had been demonstrated for buildings like schools of surgeries, a sum would be allocated according to prescriptive criteria with little regard for how they might interact with other social services. Under the Single Regeneration Budget, various activities have to come together with some proven benefit in doing so and rather than having funds allocated of right, bids are competitive. Often funds from this budget can be combined with awards from the National Lottery and occasionally from the European Fund for Reconstruction and Development, which greatly increases the scope of public projects.

Several effects can be traced to these changes. As bids have to be hetergeneous and tailored to particular local needs, more control of their conception lies at a local level rather than in government departments. There is, consequently, a new breed of client, who is responsible for co-ordinating such projects, finding various sources of funds, and acting as a champion. They have to act in part as entrepreneurs and in part as public servants, which is exactly the cusp on which architecture lies, between the private interests of a client and an obligation to a wider public. As high design standards are essential for success, architecture becomes an explicit part of the bids; indeed it is sometimes the only unifying point between different aims and ambitions. Despite the possibility of crippling bureaucracy, these arrangements are generally beneficial to architecture; architects have the opportunity to contribute to social provision rather than merely to react and give built form to existing policy. The contrast with 30 years ago, when architects had a safer but more subservient role, could not be greater.

Numerous projects in this book benefit from these new arrangements. Allford Hall Monaghan Morris's bus station in Walsall, a rundown town near Birmingham, and Haworth Tompkins's 'hot house' at Coin Street on London's South Bank both show how the possibility of amalgamating different sources of funding can encourage innovative design for public facilities. AHMM have breathed new life into a building type which had become utilitarian and uninviting, while Haworth Tompkins are working with their client Coin Street Community Builders, one of the most successful of the bodies emerge as providers of public buildings, to devise a new type of public institution, combining leisure and educational facilities. Shed KM's series of projects which created Concert Square in Liverpool show how an entire civic quarter might come about through a mixture of commercial activity and public funds, opening up a new public space within a tight grid of warehouses with routes into existing thoroughfares. Stephen Hodder's consummate adaptation of modernist forms indicates how architecture might serve new and traditional academic institutions, at St Catherine's College Oxford, and the Centenary Building in Salford.

Especially where art, cultural and educational facilities are included, funds from the National Lottery often supplement those directly specifically toward regeneration. Caruso St John's art gallery, also in Walsall, is another example of how an existing building type can be transformed. Sensitive to the works in the permanent collection, flexible for travelling exhibitions, stressing education, its most notable aspect is nonetheless its dramatic presence in Walsall, fronting a new square and an expanded canal basin. Richard Murphy's Arts Centre in Dundee brings together an unusual mix of local and international artistic media, from textiles to cinema, with a fully equipped gallery for travelling exhibitions. Bauman Lyons's South Promenade in Bridlington integrates art directly into the architectural, not forcing an existing concept of art to sit on an existing concept of public realm, but offering a new configuration of both.

If architecture lies somewhere in the spectrum between fine art and engineering-scale infrastructure, several firms operate at the extremes. Weston Williamson's reworking of the complicated and poorly co-ordinated elements which make up London Bridge underground station – prompted by the addition of the Jubilee Line extension to the existing Northern Line – re-visits the idea of a 'kit of parts', a familiar theme in British architecture which reached its apogee in 'high tech'. They use this delicate architectural sensibility to tame the very different aesthetic of Victorian infrastructure, a maze of long tunnels. In a series of projects Birds Portchmouth Russum also show how transport infrastructure might be refined; the infrastructure they address serves the car – car parks and roads – and they evolve an imaginative iconography to render it meaningful and enjoyable, coupled with an ability to manipulate form so skilfully that the awkward curves and shapes which traffic engineers bequeath to public space are made usable.

Suggesting that in architecture no useful distinction can be made between art and infrastructure, is the work of FAT. They consciously draw on the visual irony and wit which characterises the work of the young British artists loosely grouped around the collector Charles Saatchi; their applications of it in the public realm are sometimes baffling and occasionally silly, but they are intended to unsettle the balance between the familiar and the unfamiliar which is a characteristic of all large cities. Underlying their initiatives is a profound interest in visual codes and communication. Several of their projects show how even ordinary London terraced houses can be turned into a series of witty, surprising and enjoyable spaces.

A more traditional view of the relationship between art and architecture can be found in Niall McLaughlin's work. The disciplines of materials and construction help to generate forms which, for instance, might be implied in certain spatial relationships depicted in paintings. The resulting forms might express the discipline of an explicit programme, as in a monastery sacristy; or, in a tiny photographer's shack in rural Northamptonshire, the acts of model-making and construction evolved a complex form which becomes both an object in the landscape and an enclosure for viewing nature.

Eric Parry also uses tectonic and constructional disciplines as a starting point for architectural expression. Each component has a particular nature which finds significance in its relationship to other parts. But his architecture is not a cipher for construction or structure, it also suggests relationships between different spaces, the people who use them and the activities which take place in them – between inanimate forms, surfaces and materials and human perceptions. Incorporating new and existing forms, they establish a dialogue between history and the present. Most redolent are Foundress Court, a large but subtle addition to the precinct of Pembroke College, one of Cambridge's oldest, and the monumental spike and visitors centre in Southwark, at the south end of London Bridge. Inclining masonry at this angle is surreal, part silent sentinel over the 26 million people who pass it every year, and part totem which suggests the ephemeral qualities of modern urban life as it changes as different faces catch different lights during the course of the day.

The proximity of Parry's Spike to Weston Williamson's remodelling of the adjacent underground station is a coincidence. Yet the contrast between them is a harbinger of the way British architects of their generation, in a wide variety of ways and serving the differing needs of numerous clients, might engage with urban topography and infrastructure more closely than at any time since cities took on their present form and the infrastructure was built in the 19th century. Here is a hint of how architecture, with a broader agenda coming from new approaches to education, and new opportunities from re-configuring its public role, might address the social forces which are encouraging the better use of existing urban buildings and sites, and which is slowly making Britain's largest cities – London, Manchester, Leeds, Liverpool – enjoyable places to be.

This book only includes one of the numerous restaurants which are, perhaps, the most prolific architectural effects of this trend. But Belgo's in Ladbroke Grove in London is probably the finest and least clichéd example. Designed by Foreign Office Architects, its folding, warping form is a tiny indication of their massive Yokohama Ferry Terminal, itself almost large enough to be a city in itself and certainly containing many of the most obvious and difficult urban functions. Conceived for a site in Japan by a firm whose roots lie across the world, its influences are necessarily broader than the sketch of the British context which this introduction attempts. But it shows in extreme form how the milieu of young architects in Britain has intellectual and operational horizons well beyond parochial national boundaries.

Allford Hall Monaghan Morris London

Having four partners allows Allford Hall Monaghan Morris to pursue a very wide agenda: their work ranges across public and private development, housing, leisure, health care, transport and education, in both urban and rural locations. They engage these different types and contexts with a series of architectural themes, including enhancements to the public realm where the programme allows, innovations in environmental strategy, and inclusion of artworks and graphics.

Above all is a commitment to buildings which are legible in construction and appearance. This varies according to building type: legibility in the Walsall bus station, for example, comes from clearly defined and easy patterns of use; for a housing development at Dalston in East London legibility comes through a bold chequerboard composition which gives the private building a public presence, and which is carried through to the division of the window bars.

Their plans express a different sort of clarity. In simple terms they are logical and consistent to suit function. This becomes an aid to composition, as in the almost Beaux-Arts axiality of the school at Great Notley. It also contributes to a strategy for handling urban sites and refurbishments, where they often see their interventions as completing or repairing an existing location. Walsall bus station is the most comprehensive example. Its design is essentially a large roof sitting on minimal structural trees; where enclosed buildings are needed, they take the form of cabins within the forest. It synthesises the demands of transport with the regeneration of the town centre. It has a clear, functional logic, but it is also part of a larger ambition. On a smaller scale is the Morelands site just to the north of the City of London where relatively minor improvements to surfaces, signage and access points create a completely different reading of what were run down light industrial blocks and has become a thriving community of small businesses.

Underlying all their designs is a profound belief in the efficacy of the language, forms and social aims of modernism for improving urban, living and working environments for the 21st century – provided that the pragmatic constraints of programme and site are respected.

Croydon Medical Centre,
London

An exercise in how a modernist formal language of planes,
volumes and strong colours
might occupy a prominent
corner site in suburban South
London.

Street facade

Broadgate Club, London

A ground floor fit out in a
contemporary office building,
Allford Hall Monaghan Morris's
design, in collaboration with
graphic designer Morag
Myerscough, used graphics
and colour-coding, including a
translucent blue wall illuminated from behind, to demark
clear routes through the
ritualised activities of a health
club.

15

Walsall Bus Station

A competition-winning design for a new bus station in a town with 260,000 residents within the Birmingham conurbation. It has a giant concrete roof punctuated with roof lights, supported on structural trees placed to suit the flow of buses and pedestrians, and the need to display information. Its function is essential for Walsall's regeneration strategy, because it improves access to the central area without increasing car traffic, and the building becomes an integral part of the town's public spaces. A new square in front of the church is part of the scheme.

Walsall Bus Station: the roof takes shape. Giant oculi pierce the heavy roof which rests on minimal columns, leaving the ground plane for buses and pedestrians.

Ground floor plan

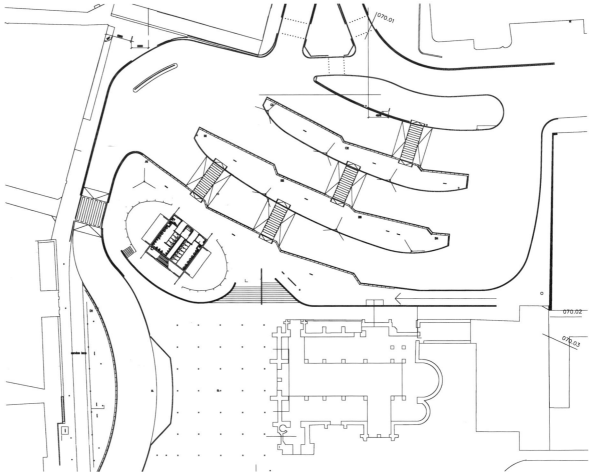

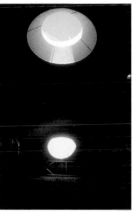

Night time view

From ground level, the roof
lights are oculuses.

The roof lights are cast into
the roof.

Interior view: as a public space
it works by the beneficial
placement of function rather
than coercive routes or spaces.

Great Notley Primary School

Allford Hall Monaghan Morris won a competition promoted by Esssex County Council and the Design Council for an energy-efficient 'sustainable' school. A single pre-stressed plywood roof opens to provide as much natural light as possible; a central courtyard means almost all spaces have an outside window and creates negative pressure to draw air from the outside walls for natural ventilation. Its form responds to the rural site; the principal classrooms are on the lower, wider and more private south front, while the sharper northern end lifts up to mark its presence in the village; under it is the most public function, the main hall.

The building lies long and low in the landscape, with roof projections which bring light into the deep plan.

Long section through hall to classrooms, shows the angling of the roof for daylight.

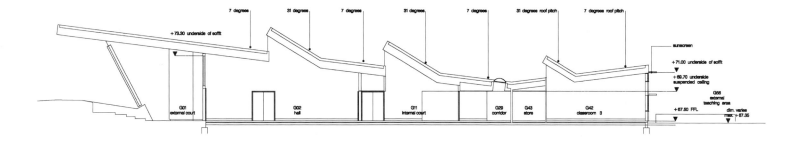

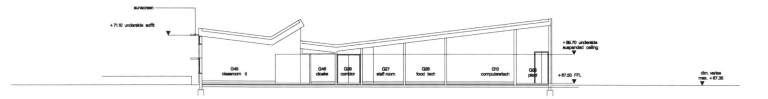

Hall interior

The sweeping roof lends
variety to the central hall.

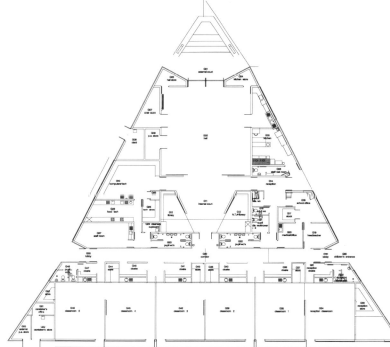

Ground floor plan

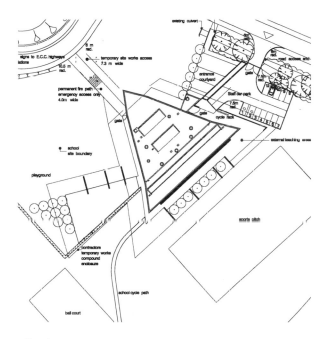

Site plan

South front

View from south east: the
cantilevered canopy marks the
children's entrance.

Peabody Trust Housing,
Dalston Lane, London

A scheme of 18 2-bed, six 1-bed flats and retail units for an innovative provider of low cost housing, it takes the typical form of its neighbours in inner East London, residential units set back and above a plinth of shops. A mixture of bold and subtle devices distinguish it and adapt it better to its uses: among the former is the chequerboard patterning of the outer facades; among the latter is the treatment of the staircase, decreasing in width towards the top and lit by rooflights to avoid the claustrophobia small staircases can cause. The strong chequerboard and single-pitch roof create a hard public face; inside are balconies which allow for a layering between communal and private spaces.

Three storeys of apartments rest on a single floor of shops. The chequerboard and fenestration patterns create a strong counterpoint.

First floor plan: 1-bedroom flats on the outer faces.

Sections: through flats (top) and staircases (bottom).

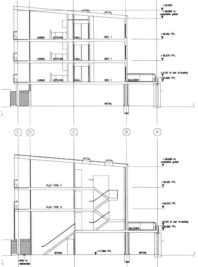

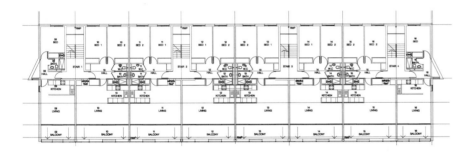

The rear elevation opens up with balconies and large windows: a more intimate and factural face than the stylisations of the street front.

Living room interior. The monopitch roof gives the top floor living rooms extra height.

Conversion of Morelands, London

A group of light industrial workshops in Clerkenwell, Central London, which Allford Hall Monaghan Morris have converted for office use, adding means of escape and access, and opening up alleys and archways.

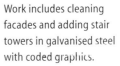

Work includes cleaning facades and adding stair towers in galvanised steel with coded graphics.

Housing, Birmingham

Ongoing projects include an innovative city centre housing development for single people in Birmingham. Two wings around a courtyard are linked by walkways.

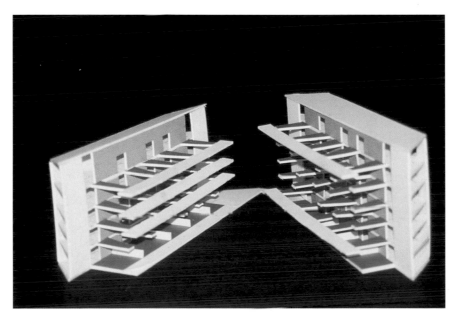

Exploded image

Bauman Lyons Leeds

Bauman Lyons are based in Leeds, and much of their work is in the industrial cities of northern England. These cities are where the industrial revolution started, but they have had mixed fortunes in attracting new industries to replace the old declining ones. Each retains a strong civic identity, but many lack the means to develop public resources and infrastructure to stimulate economic regeneration.

Bauman Lyons's work is an architectural response to this condition. Their approach evolves between two poles: one is to present art objects in an attractive and accessible way – public funds for regeneration, especially from the National Lottery, often require cultural, educational and leisure facilities; the other pole is a commitment to large scale improvements to the public realm, often through creating new public spaces or dramatically improving old ones. As many of these projects also involve public art installations, the two poles often come together and in turn raise another issue: the boundaries between clearly defined institutions housed in discrete buildings – such as the galleries endowed by 19th century philanthropists which are common in the northern cities – and the public realm.

In several recent projects Bauman Lyons have started to investigate what form new institutions might take. They seek to combine leisure, cultural and educational purposes, and to avoid the rigid distinctions which traditional gallery – or college – design imposed. And in concentrating on public space their work often challenges the conventional parameters of the 'architectural project'. On one level it blurs the distinction between art and architecture, but it also attempts to claim for architecture the ground surface which has all too often fallen into the hands of transport engineers or urban planners with disastrous results.

South Promenade, Bridlington

Bridlington is a run-down seaside resort on England's north-east coast. A far-sighted and imaginative arts officer in the local council, Andrew Knight, realised that the combination of grants from the National Lottery and European Reconstruction and Development Fund could pay for a major remodelling of the seafront promenade running into a huge bay from the town's small harbour. In putting together Bauman Lyons with the sculptor Bruce Mclean and writer Mel Gooding he signalled a break with the typical gaudy vulgarity of a seaside resort: Bauman Lyons evoke a rationalism in beach huts which almost refer to Aldo Rossi, and in a hierarchy of spaces defined by Gooding's words, Mclean's sculptures and ground surface.

A careful layering and stepping of terraces gives the town a public space overlooking its greatest asset.

As the promenade runs from the harbour, it becomes less urban and more informal, until it reaches this café, the point where the promenade gives way to the wide bay.

In the interests of economy and neatness, objects often have a double function. Here a bin is also a seat.

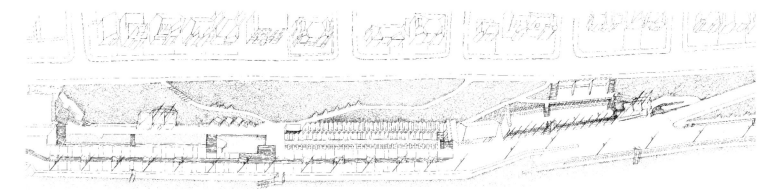

Axonometric

Garston Public Space,
Liverpool

A scheme to create a heart for
Garston, an anonymous
suburb of Liverpool, by the
relatively simple means of
bringing order to objects for
functions which already take
place: market stalls, bus
shelters and other street
furniture. Improving the public
realm is effected not through
introducing the extraordinary,
but reinforcing the ordinary.

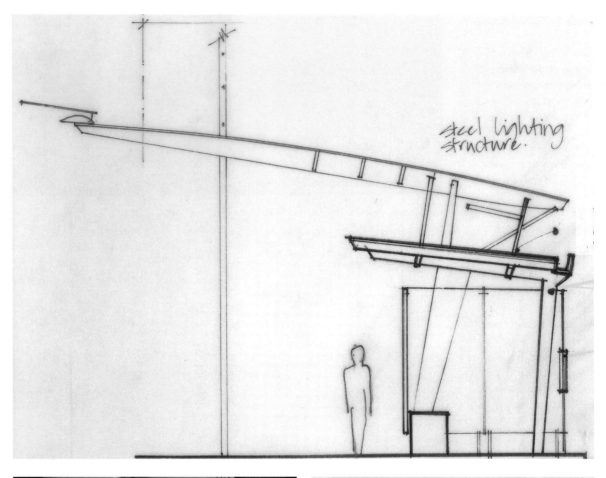

steel lighting
structure.

Section through bus stop

Design model of Garston
public space

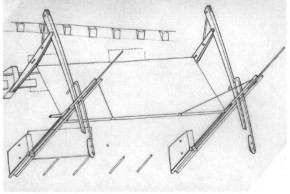

Bus shelter or market stall
with street lighting. A basic kit
of parts can be adapted for
several functions.

Ferensway Development, Hull

Bauman Lyons were among several architect members of a consortium which competed to redevelop a 20 hectare site, formerly railway marshalling yards, on the edge of the centre of Hull. Their remit was to reinforce the public space. The overall masterplan sought to create a street pattern which replicates the character of Hull's historic and now pedestrianised centre, and to provide a gateway to the city's western suburbs. A new square would have doubled as an outdoor performance space, outside a theatre for the innovative Hull Truck theatre company, whose resident playwright, John Godber, is the second most produced dramatist in English.

Performance space

Masterplan

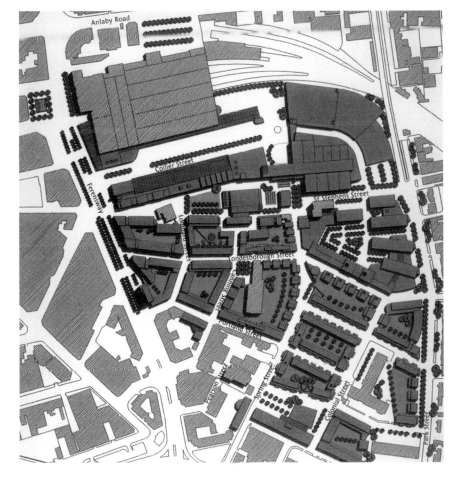

Leeds Arts Quarter

A project to create a 'Carnival' Square on an empty piece of wasteland overlooking central Leeds. It will combine indoor and outdoor performance spaces of varying formality. It responds to the cultures of the numerous immigrant communities in the area, and on its past – a concert venue will be created out of a distinguished but derelict 1930s working men's club, organisations which were once an integral part of working class Leeds life.

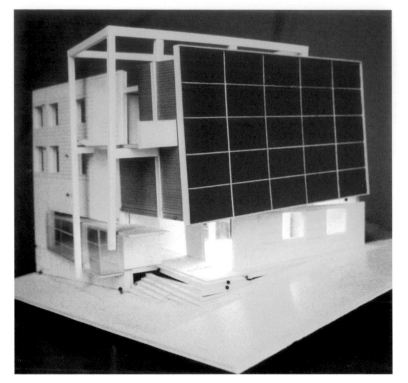

View into the foyer, proposed concert venue

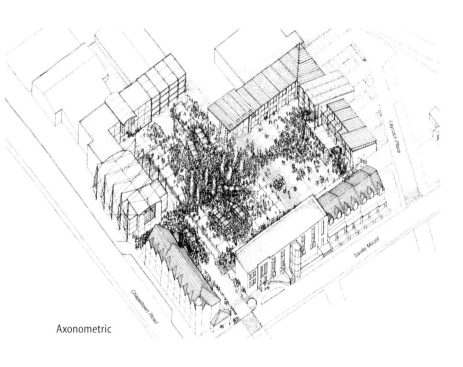

Axonometric

View of the side of the proposed concert venue

A view over the site

Displaying Art Objects

Bauman Lyons exhibition projects range from the 200 hectare Yorkshire Sculpture Park, to the design of display stands for the National Museum of Photography, Film and Television in Bradford.

Yorkshire Sculpture Park: view with Henry Moore sculpture in the foreground. An initiative to take art out of the gallery and relate it to nature.

Display stands at the National Museum of Photography, Film and Television, designed to optimise viewing for all visitors.

Subway to the National Museum of Photography, Film and Television: an ordinary pedestrian subway is taken over by a hidden projector system, making a continually changing display of images on the walls.

Much of Bauman Lyons' work devises new relationships between art and the public. Their work for the National Museum of Film and Television in Bradford includes an installation in a public subway leading to the museum, which projects photographic images onto the tunnel walls, and this installation for an exhibition on the history of photography. Subject matter, curatorial intention and design are all intended to re-configure the way art is seen, and to allow viewers to engage with the exhibits in a variety of ways.

Birds Portchmouth Russum   London

Birds Portchmouth Russum is so far the only significant practice to have emerged from the office of James Stirling and Michael Wilford. All three of the London-based partners, Andrew Birds, Richard Portchmouth and Mike Russum – Karl Jensen is based in New York – worked for Stirling Wilford, before winning a competition in 1989 for a car park on the edge of Chichester, a small, unspoilt city on the south coast of England with a Roman street pattern, streets lined with 18th century facades on older houses, and dominated by a fine cathedral of Norman and Gothic construction.

Most similar projects in Britain face two large problems. Planning authorities restrict designs near sites of historic interest to historical pastiche, while car parks are rarely accorded much attention. But BPR's approach to architecture helps them to engage with these challenges directly. Like their mentor James Stirling, they use the spatial, formal and constructional attributes of buildings to create meaning and dialogue: the wall is both a reference to the city wall and something to conceal the cars as well as a pedestrian route; the stair towers refer to traditional turrets, but their colour coding helps motorists to locate their cars. Meaning and a dialogue with place add to the old modernist duality of form and function.

The car park was a spur to developing a sequence of projects which investigate the problem of traffic in cities. In Croydon, a dreary suburban centre in South London, they proposed using existing car parks for a series of leisure activities, combining an imaginative efficiency of use with exuberant enjoyment; commissioned by the Department of Transport, they elaborate on the area's maritime and industrial connections. At Canning Town, a beached ship recalls its past as the transportational hub of an Empire; at Dagenham, British home of the Ford Motor Company, the motorway pylons assume the form of spark plugs. And in Belfast, perhaps the most emotive of depressed industrial cities, BPR look at practical and sensitive ways of creating usable and meaningful urban spaces within a zone killed by a motorway flyover.

Avenue de Chartres Car Park,
Chichester

A car park becomes as much a
part of a historic city as its
magnificent cathedral; the city
wall evolves into a pedestrian
route and the edge of the car
park, recalling the historic use
of city walls as promenades
and combining legibility with
function, and history with a
strategy for handling cars.

A pedestrian bridge between
the car park and the historic
centre forms a new gateway to
the city.

Site plan

The historic core and new car
park: the design is not just a
simple extension of a Roman-
gridded city, but relates pre-
modern and post-modern
urbanism.

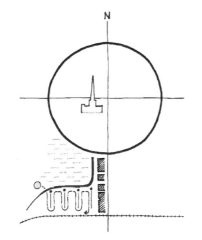

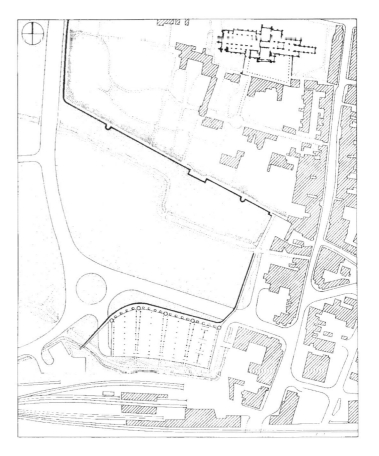

The stair turrets are illuminated at night, each is coded with a different colour to aid legibility and orientation.

The wall is both a boundary and pedestrian route, designed for easy passage or for lingering to enjoy the view, and to facilitate finding the right car.

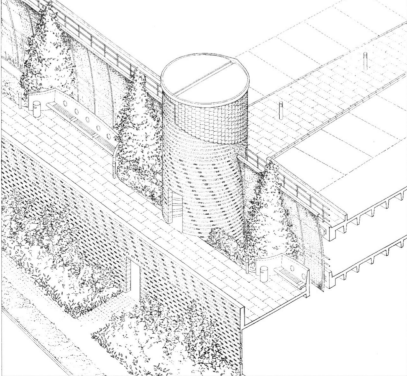

Laganside masterplan, Belfast

Insensitive urban development intensified Belfast's social and political ills, and all militated against the evolution of public space and public life. BPR's masterplan for a site on the River Lagan would have placed a car park under a motorway flyover, edging it with buildings which would have created a new square and a pedestrian link to the city centre. The intensity of the particular location suggests a strategy for a generic urban problem, recognising the reality of car use and re-establishing public space in the vicinity of a flyover.

An urban proposal that accepts the reality of the motor car, and enhances life for pedestrians.

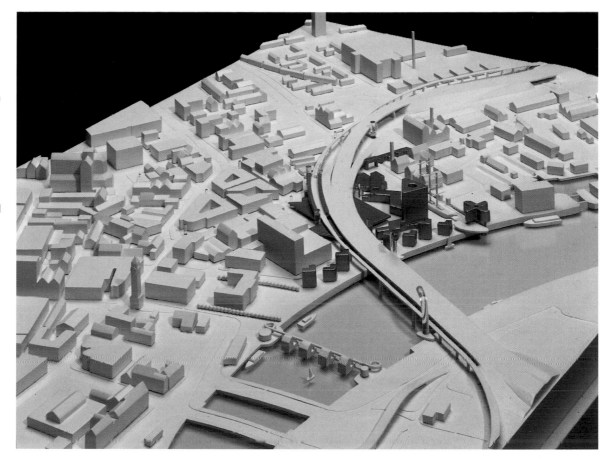

Corporation Square, a new riverside space overlooked by the historic customs house and new buildings which shield the motorway. The ship refers to Belfast's maritime past.

Left: Erosion of Belfast's urban fabric – decades of insensitive urban planning destroyed the city's dense unity.

Right: Restoring Belfast's urban fabric – BPR's scheme would have recreated a link between the waterfront and the city centre and created a new space with strongly defined edges and a romantic centrepiece.

1960

1980

1995

A 13 Road Improvements

The A 13 is a main road leading out of London to the east. The vast but largely empty docks recall the area's past as the transport hub of a huge commercial empire and London's largest industrial area: modern roads seem designed to move people through it as fast as possible with no indication of history, a measure of its decline. BPR's improvements bridge the gap between historical associations and modern realities, with a piece of street furniture and a few set-pieces which evoke the past in a way which is legible even to passengers in a speeding car.

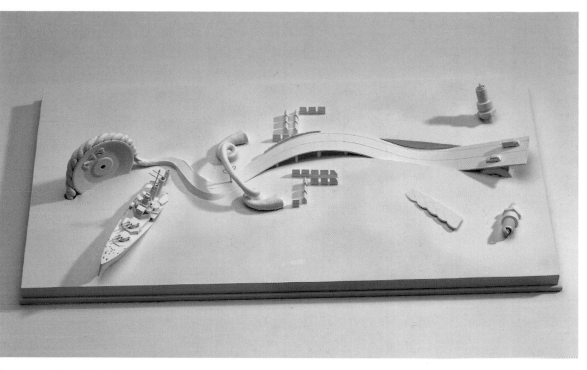

Concept model: outsize relics of an industrial past prevent this outsize post-industrial dystopia from becoming unduly pessimistic.

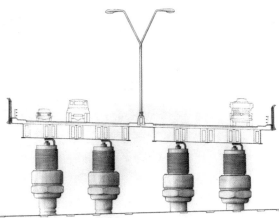

Beckton flyover is near the Ford factory at Dagenham: its pylons are giant spark plugs. The streetlamps vary in height according to the number of twists: passing them rapidly gives the effect of a bird flapping its wings.

Canning Town flyover: a beached ship recalls the time when water rather than road transport dominated.

Croydromia, London

Croydon is an outer London suburb ringed with ugly concrete car parks. BPR's idea was to use their rooftops for evening leisure purposes when they would otherwise be empty, and exploiting their over-sized structures. The Fairfield drome would provide small scale enclosed cinemas during the day; at night they would open to double the seating with the gas filled screen floating above. The culture drome would offer a performance space and a multi-level foyer linking to and enlivening an under-used square.

At night the Culture Drome would bring life to street as well as roof level.

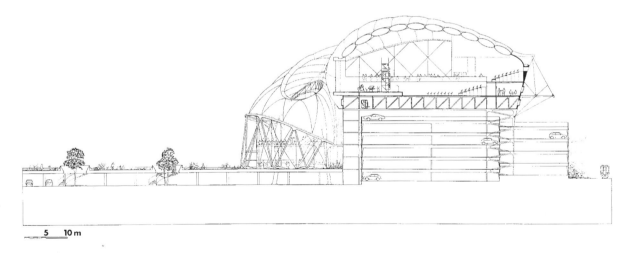

Section through Culture Drome, a fabric roofed performance space and foyer.

5   10 m

34

The Fairfield Drome provides small enclosed cinemas by day, and larger, open air ones at night when demand would be heaviest.

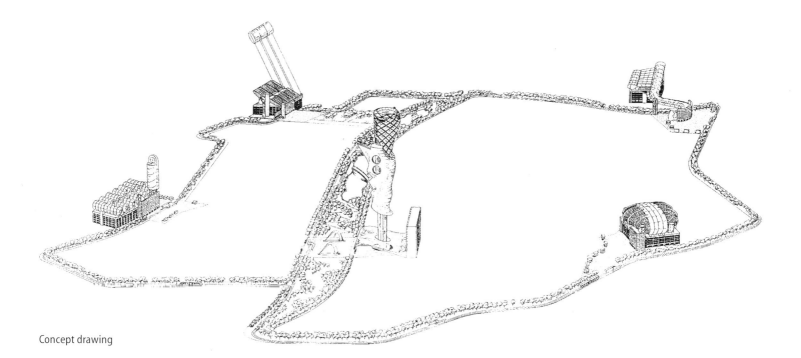

Concept drawing

Footbridges

In two footbridge proposals, BPR explore how the language and form of construction might intermesh with movement patterns to create meaning out of specific circumstances.

Hadrian's Bridge between Scotland and England: construction celebrates difference rather than homogeneity.

Plan of Hadrian's Bridge between Scotland and England: the sinuous forms reluctantly meet and each ends up facing the other direction – the two countries' relationship has not always been easy.

Plashet School footbridge
joins two schools on adjacent
sites in East London together.
Their different histories,
traditions and architecture are
recognised in the reverse
curvature.

Caruso St John London

Caruso St John are the austere representatives of at least two traditions: they develop a formal and specifically English approach of using materials and components in their plain, as-found state, which certainly goes back to the Smithsons and some might trace to the stern and severe Gothic Revivalists such as William Butterfield. But Caruso St John are among the most international of young British architects; their attention to the specific character of materials, details and forms takes them close to the European minimalism of Herzog and de Meuron and Peter Zumthor. This context helps to explain the elemental nature of their architecture; they lavish enormous attention to ensuring that planes are read as planes, volumes as volumes, and to distinguish what is old from what is new.

Their most significant project so far is an art gallery in Walsall, an industrial town near Birmingham. It achieves an enormous force through the architectural expression of the contrast between the domestic-scale, side-lit rooms which house the permanent, Garman Ryan collection of small works by artists from Dürer to Freud, and the double height, clerestory-lit spaces which can house almost any temporary exhibition. Spaces have a specific intensity. But because there are so many routes between them, each visit could be different, suggesting a multiplicity of readings for the works, and their relationship to each other, to what is permanent and what is temporary.

The exterior compresses these complex relationships to a purely architectural analogue. At a glance it is a mute, grey tower in an unprepossessing urban location; inspected more carefully, the positioning of windows within the terracotta-tile-clad wall becomes deliberate, suggesting the crafting of the interior space without revealing it. And by eroding a corner for the entrance directly under the highest part of the building, it takes on an almost surreal air – this structural feat required more than 100 ties concealed in the ground. Yet it also invites free movement onto the new public square in front of the gallery while clearly distinguishing interior from exterior: art is accessible, but the experience of looking at it is different to shopping.

Later projects, including competition entries for the Centre for Contemporary Arts in Rome and an extension to a 1970s school in Wörgl, Austria, develop some of these themes. The Rome arts centre had a far more diverse brief than Walsall: their scheme matched that diversity with a conscious variation of new and old buildings, rough and smooth finishes, ambiguities and juxtapositions, just as Rome itself, through its inconsistencies, is greater than the sum of its parts. The Wörgl school extension responds to the rigour of the structuralist approach of the existing building but avoids its insensitivity to function: pre-fabricated timber panels act as structure, surface and formers of space, in contrast to the division between structure and lightweight partitions in the existing school. The extension also includes a stoa to mediate between the public and private spaces.

Walsall Art Gallery
and Public Square

This tower-like building soars above the roofs of Walsall, a midlands town near Birmingham, relating it to the other towers of the town hall and church. The form creates a series of discrete floor plates which are individually designed for their purpose, either displaying the small scale works of the permanent Garman Ryan Collection, or temporary shows, with galleries finished and lit to be suitable for any exhibition. Visitors can move through the building in a variety of ways, encouraging exploration of the experience of seeing art and development of particular relationships with the collection. There is also a generous foyer which relates to the new public square designed by artists Catherine Yass and Richard Wentworth.

The gallery tower hovers enigmatically above Walsall.

Reticent but evocative, the gallery has an austerity which distinguishes it from its neighbours and invites contemplation.

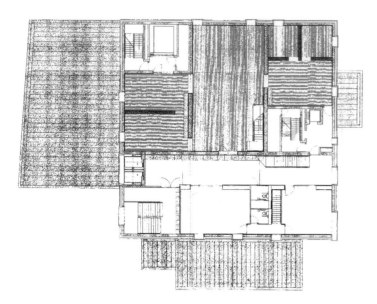

First floor plan

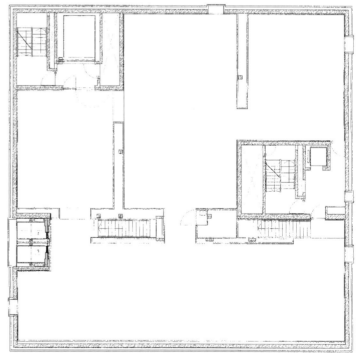

Fourth floor plan, restaurant
and conference room

Ground floor plan, foyer
and shop

Third floor plan, the temporary
exhibition galleries

The tower form adds to its civic presence. Grey terracotta tiles clad a concrete frame.

Section through foyer: Garman Ryan Galleries are on the first and second floors, exhibition galleries on the third floor and a restaurant and conference room on the fourth floor.

The temporary exhibition gallery on the third floor is large and high enough to take most travelling exhibitions; its clerestory lighting allows many different layouts.

Section through the circulation core

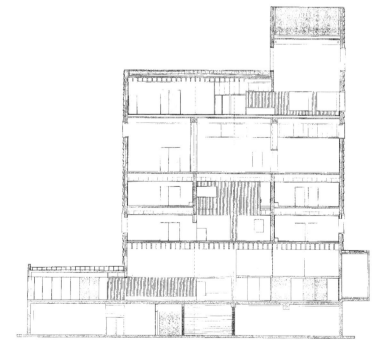

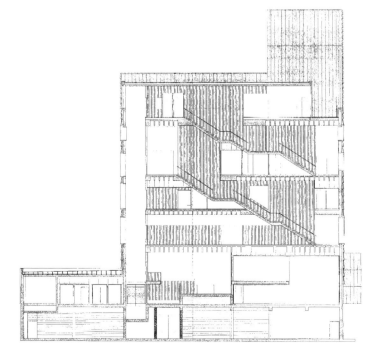

Facade detail

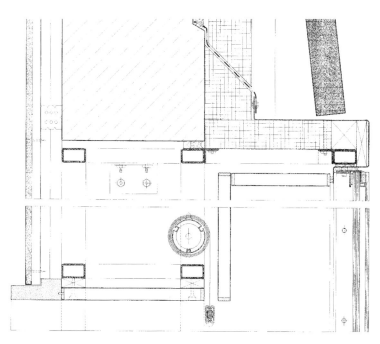

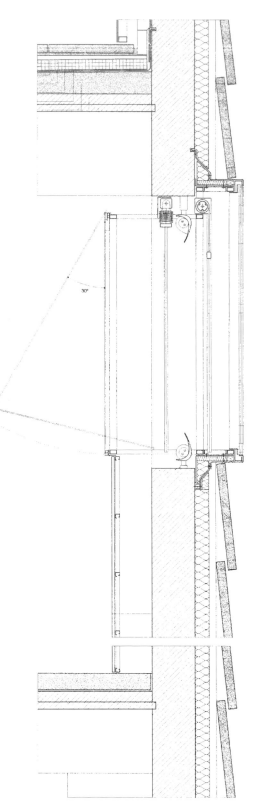

Window head detail, Garman
Ryan Galleries. The intimate
feel of these galleries comes
from their domestic scale and
because they are side-lit.

Clerestory window detail,
temporary exhibition gallery.
The details are carefully
designed to modulate day-
light; artificial lights are in
the ceiling.

School at Wörgl, Austria

Competition entry for an extension to a 1970s school. The additions are as rigorous as the structuralist discipline of the original building, but their rigour is less abstract and more related to the processes of teaching and learning. The timber wall panels themselves contribute to the character of the classrooms; in the original this comes from a contrast between structure and infill; and a new stoa relates the school to its surroundings.

Perspective looking toward the stoa.

Section through extension, original seen in elevation.

Centre for Contemporary Arts, Rome

A competition entry for a new arts centre. The design reflects the heterogeneity both of the collection of existing and new buildings, and of the probable exhibitions. Overall concern for finishes and surface creates an abstract unity.

Model photograph of part of the existing galleries for the permanent collection: like art, the structure speaks for itself.

Sections: the scheme created a wide variety of different spaces.

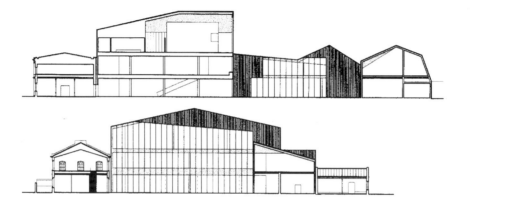

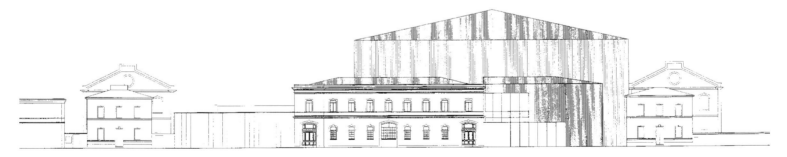

Elevation to Via Guido Reni: contrast between new and old is a metaphor for traditional and contemporary art – different but not incompatible.

Model photograph of new
galleries for temporary
exhibitions, clad in mill-
finished corrugated stainless
steel. Careful distortions
differentiate their otherwise
similar forms from the existing
buildings.

Ground floor plan

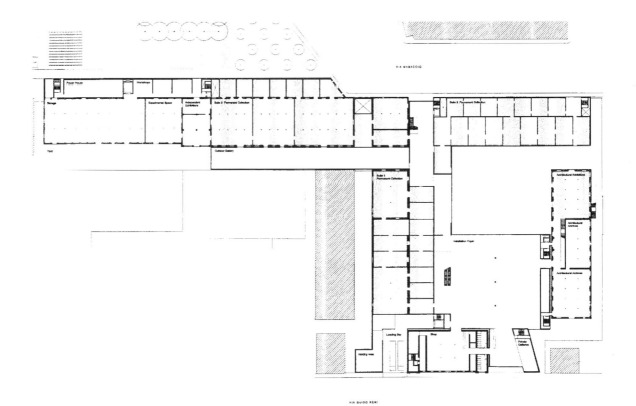

Patrick Davies London

Finding latent potential through strong formal interventions in unpromising locations is a consistent theme in Patrick Davies' varied projects. His experience gives him a wide range of sources to draw on: he worked for the Richard Rogers Partnership on Lloyd's of London, studied at the Harvard Graduate School of Design for a year when Richard Meier's influence was strong, and investigated Italian Rationalism and Baroque architecture while a scholar at the British School in Rome.

Each of these influences can be traced in his projects, but in a synthesis that eludes easy labels. The layered facades and tantalising glimpses of different volumes behind perhaps refers most obviously to Meier, but the careful planning of his buildings, creating formal spaces within irregular sites, owes much to the baroque. His details may display an influence from Rogers, but they are rarely such demonstrative ends-in-themselves as might be found in full-blown high tech.

Several projects show how his balance between an abstract formal language and pragmatic manipulation of circumstance might evolve urban forms and building types. The dramatic structures for advertising hoardings generate income for otherwise dead urban sites which can be devoted to improving their localities, but they are also exercises in a particular formal language – how far can a steel tubular arch span, or at what angle might it incline? The Kings Waterfront housing development in Liverpool is a functionally more complex and formally richer attempt to create a new presence on an empty urban site near the austere Albert Dock which houses Stirling Wilford's Tate Gallery of the North.

St David's Hotel in Cardiff, itself drawing on several unbuilt hotel projects, is the most comprehensive example. At one level it is an act of urban regeneration, one of the new uses being brought in to revive a derelict dock area, but it also develops a new formal typology for luxury hotels. The public spaces of a restaurant, bar, function rooms and a health club occupy the wide, spreading base, while bedrooms are located in two wings above. Joining these two parts is a high, curving atrium capped by a whimsical and eye-catching roof. It is a building whose form is its own advertisement, and where the practical relationships of the parts to each other generates the sense of well-being which a luxury hotel needs. Its form is sufficient so that it does not need the gilded decoration or opulent furniture normally used to denote luxury.

78 Old Street, London

A 4,000 sq m office block in London's Clerkenwell district. It has narrow frontage onto Old Street, but its T-shape plan widens to the rear, a configuration which is resolved with a tightly planned street facade: a small glass-fronted atrium becomes transparent at night, allowing glimpses into the empty office space, almost in the manner of a 17th century Dutch peep box.

Street facade

Agincourt Road Offices, London

A small backland site in fringe location is organised around a spinal street, overlooked by dramatic and intriguing staircores. Recalling the grouping around staircases of rooms in Oxford and Cambridge colleges, they take up the site deformations and have space for photocopiers and casual meetings, allowing the office space to be extremely effcient.

View into staircases

ECME Factory, Oporto

A project for an electrical goods factory in Oporto, Portugal, for a subsidiary of General Electric. Its size and repetition of elements meant that many parts were to be custom-designed, notably a the structural tree which formed one bay unit.

Advertising Structures

Davies has designed several structures for advertisements on prominent roadside sites. Often their awkward shape stimulates an innovative structural solution, adding an architectural image to the advertising ones, and opening possiblities for a relationship between business and public interests in the public realm: the structures often yield a rent for local councils for land which would otherwise be derelict.

An advertising structure at Heathrow Airport uses the value of passers-by to improve the public realm.

View of the advertisting structure at the south end of Wandsworth Bridge in London: a modern structure carries messages which can easily be taken in from a passing car.

The roundabout at the south end of Wandsworth Bridge in South London is one of the busiest in the city.

A structure on Cromwell Road, West London.

St David's Hotel, Cardiff

Wales had no five star hotels until the St David's Hotel was finished in 1999. It is part of a major redevelopment of the Cardiff Docks, introducing leisure, cultural, political and commercial activities to the redundant port: Zaha Hadid's opera house would have been opposite and Richard Rogers' Welsh Assembly will be nearby. The hotel is also a serious attempt to generate a sense of luxury and quality from its exploitation of a magnificent promontary site, and the use of modernist forms and rational planning. The rooms, which are essentially similar, are in the upper floors and their discipline tightly expressed. Large more public spaces like the bar, health club, restaurant and function rooms occupy the freer form podium, and the two systems resolve in the atrium, under the spectacular roof canopy.

View from across the bay

The client, Sir Rocco Forte, wanted the entrance to be a simple composition with reception to one side, concierge to the other, and lifts ahead.

Bedroom decor avoids the tassles and frills that normally denote luxury.

The main entrance is on the
landside.

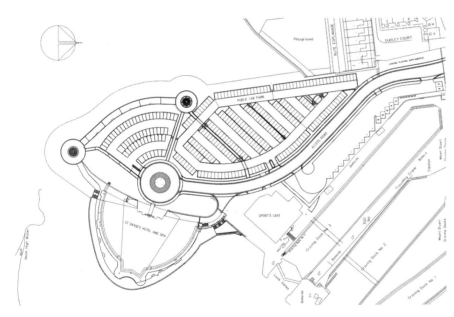

View from side

The site is on a promontory
with water on three sides.

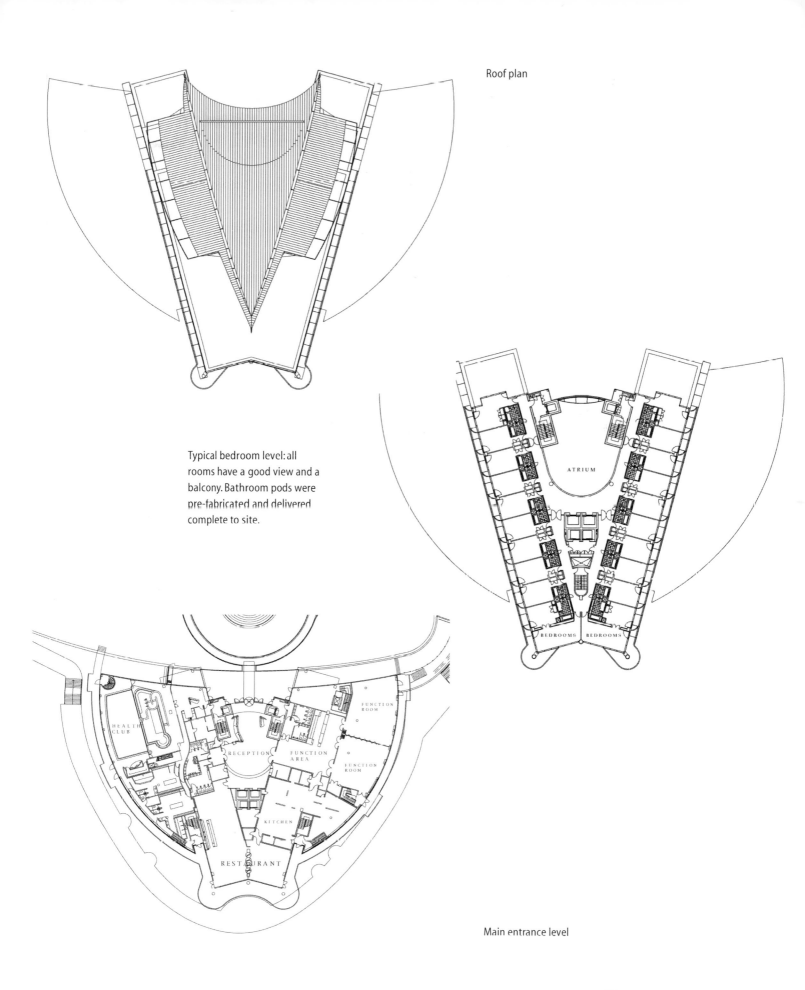

Roof plan

Typical bedroom level: all rooms have a good view and a balcony. Bathroom pods were pre-fabricated and delivered complete to site.

ATRIUM

BEDROOMS BEDROOMS

HEALTH CLUB

RECEPTION

FUNCTION AREA

FUNCTION ROOM

FUNCTION ROOM

KITCHEN

RESTAURANT

Main entrance level

51

Several ongoing projects show how Davies's formal language evolves around a wide range of functions. A health club for Virgin Active in London adapts the structural system developed for the ECME factory – a roof light over the tree; a housing development in former docklands in Liverpool develops the theme weaving layering and volumes, in particular in the balconies which derive from St David's Hotel; a sports centre for the University of London Union, where the main sports hall volume sits within a filigree poché of ancillary spaces; and an office in Byng Street in London's Docklands – an essay in how a large (54,000 sq m, 20 storey) building might respond to the history, context and use of the area.

Virgin Active

The Liverpool housing scheme develops the theme of a large residential building, mediated by careful layering of facades.

Typical floor plan

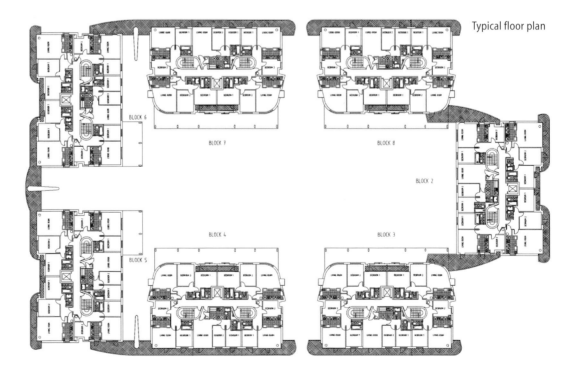

University of London Union,
Sports Hall

Office building, Byng street,
London: Between the two
blocks is a 15 storey atrium,
and the lower block is topped
by a sky lobby.

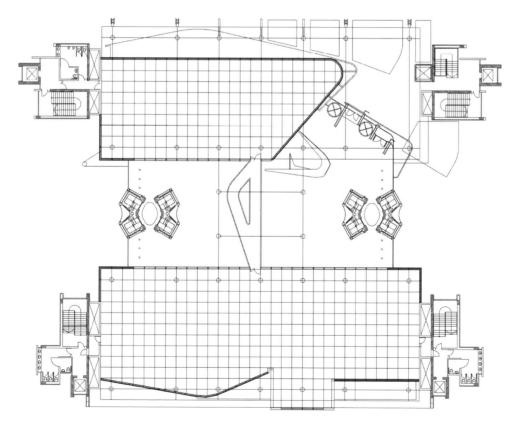

Ground floor plan: the wedge
shape building diminishes as it
rises.

FAT London

FAT (Fashion Architecture Taste) came to prominence in the early 1990s with a series of projects which explored the interface between art, architecture, and public space and private institutions. The most extensive of these was to hire numerous bus stop shelters across London (they have to be hired in bulk), and to modify their appearance. Some they did themselves; for others they commissioned different architects and artists. The result was a sequence of interventions which questioned conventional distinctions between art, architecture and advertising, and between the space of the streets and of the 'gallery'.

Language and codings embodied in conventional objects, and the way they could be manipulated, emerged as areas for speculation. A polemical project, the Anti-Oedipal House, explored in formal and iconographic terms the age-old tension between parents and children within the context of suburban housing: at the same time, the real examples of those notional children would have been affected by the growth of 'clubbing', and might have visited the Leisure Lounge in London, or Swindon's Brunel Rooms where clubbers could immerse themselves in a space which has the indeterminate attributes of a swimming pool, or 'chill out' in a room which deliberately evokes a 1950s living room. In spatial terms they use layers to create boundaries, while their iconographies explicitly explore means of communicating rather than attempt to be 'heroically original'.

FAT's interests have many origins. One strand reaches back to the Independent Group of artists who found artistic value in the everyday objects of early consumerism of the 1950s; another lies in the gestural tactics of the Situationists – both tendencies also influenced Archigram in the 1960s. Most striking and unusual among British architects for whom Post Modernism still represents a threat, FAT seriously take on the challenges which Robert Venturi set out in Complexity and Contradiction, and with Denise Scott Brown, who herself studied with members of the Independent Group, in Learning from Las Vegas.

A series of recent projects makes this apparent. For the Kessels Kramer advertising agency in Amsterdam, they converted a 19th century Gothic church into an office, enjoying the contrast between the austere atmosphere and insipid detail of the original with their playful interventions which superficially denote beach, garden and sport, but also imply divisions between tasks within the office. Several domestic projects develop similar themes. An old chapel in North London has an interior clad with rough wooden planks which might normally make a garden fence, and a typical terraced house in South London, remodelled for a couple who are both writers, has two distinct writing spaces and a new living room which is partly double-height, interwoven with other spaces within the house, enriched with deliberately outscale classical fragments, and where the presence of books is always felt. Owing as much to Soane as Venturi, it indicates the potential of an approach which is more innovative than what FAT terms the nostalgia of the radical avant-garde.

The Anti-Oedipal House

A polemical project which explored the interface between the domestic and and the unfamiliar or frightening power of destructive family relationships, through formal and architectural language. Children and parents in a notional nuclear family had distinctly different parts of the house which reflected their likely needs.

Ad-site
The advertising space on London's bustops can be hired. FAT took over 50 and asked numerous artists and designers to collaborate on transforming them. One acquired a thatched roof, bringing the idealised and stereotyped notion of a country cottage to a gritty urban location.

Brunel Rooms Nightclub,
Swindon

A playful combination of easily
recognisable visual codes.

The chill out space consciously
resembles a 1950s living room.

Clubbers can imagine themselves in a swimming pool
rather than on a dance floor.

Chapel Conversion, North
London

Numerous old chapels have
been converted into homes
when they become redundant
for their original purpose. Their
large single volumes (and
often very plain architecture)
are ideal for imaginative
conversion, but few have been
subverted as much as this one.
Its interior finishes include
timber boarding, which is
generally found on sheds or
fences and denotes cosy
domesticity. It introduces a
familiar reference point, but
used in an unfamiliar way, it
offers a variety of interpreta-
tions.

Chapel interior, upper level

Section through chapel

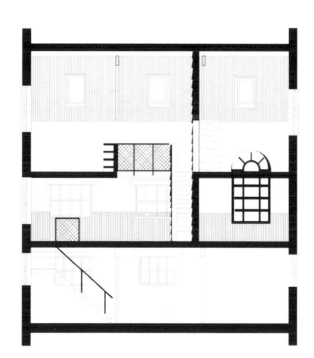

The interior retains the original
volume which contrasts with
the new colours and finishes.

House conversion,
South London

This house for two writers in South London is part of a typical London terrace. Its form, of a bay window onto the street and a front and a back room on each floor is very common, and itself a domestic 'code'. Whether on the rear facade (the front could not be touched) or in the main spaces, FAT retain enough of the original for its character always to be present, but subtly weave in other frames of reference, such as high classicism, modernist spatial effects, and the occupiers' particular interests in books, writing and convivial entertainment. Explicitly acknowledged visual codes become the mediating devices between the unforgiving restrictions of a particular building type and the activities of its occupiers.

The living room is partly double height with numerous real and apparent spaces leading off it.

Rear view, the positioning, size and shape of windows introduces an unfamiliar note into a row of monotonous back walls along the terrace.

Plan

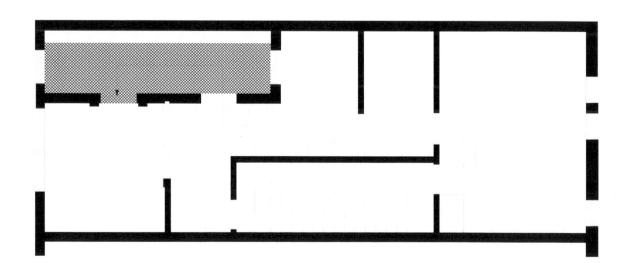

Doors open off the main bedroom to surprisingly different spaces.

Section

Kessels Kramer Advertising Agency

Advertising agents work with familiar objects and references to manipulate public opinion. FAT converted this 19th century gothic church in Amsterdam into a series of spaces for different tasks, each clearly defined by architectural fragments which explicitly refer to the sorts of commonly understood activities which advertising agents might use – football, holidays or landmarks. These are slotted between the original iron columns.

 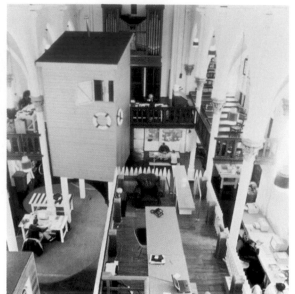

Views into the chapel

Sketches showing various options for the insertions – describing their function and their reference.

 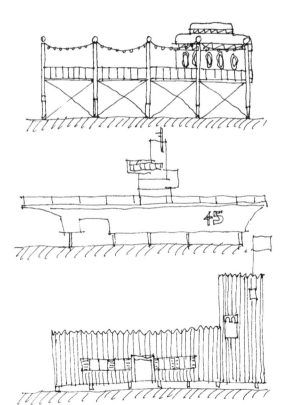

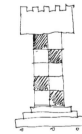 

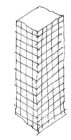  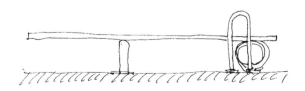

Sketch showing another option for the insertions.

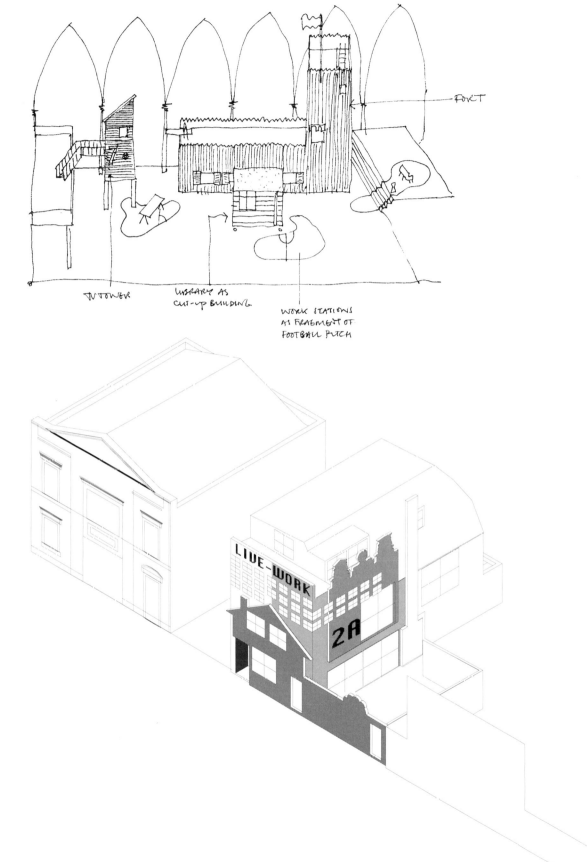

FORT

TV TOWER

LIBRARY AS
CUT-UP BUILDING

WORK STATIONS
AS FRAGMENT OF
FOOTBALL PITCH

Axonometric of proposed house and studio in East London, developing the idea of a facade which carries meaning through overt reference, with spaces for particular activities behind.

LIVE-WORK

2A

Foreign Office Architects London

Foreign Office Architects' warped and folded shapes are a powerful statement of their belief that architecture should expand its traditional intellectual concerns. Farshid Moussavi and Alejandro Zaera-Polo seek what they call 'external' constraints to establish the parameters of their practice; such an approach reverses the conventional pattern of indeterminacy within rigid though artificially defined limits, to one where architectural themes can interweave with specific external processes, such as the mobility of resources and investment.

The sensuously undulating surfaces and spaces of the Yokohama International Port Terminal are the most dramatic development of a strategy which blends structures and programmes. There may be several ground levels, which warp into a single folded plane, or part of a consistent ground might merge with wall and roof, leaving interstices for openings. As these formal transformations generally have a functional or operational purpose, the relationship between form and function assumes a determinacy of the specific condition, rather than of architectural convention. How passengers circulate through the terminal is an example.

Another illustration is in the large urban scale competition entries for the Myeong-Dong cathedral precinct in Seoul, Korea, and the harbour site in Santa Cruz, Tenerife. Working at the scale of infrastructure rather than particular buildings creates a whole series of unconventional though specific relationships, such as the way the radial streets in Santa Cruz appear to be drawn together and resolve themselves in the public levels of the pier, or the complex resolution of different elements and functions in Seoul: that these can be as ambitious as using integration as a metaphor for uniting believers and non-believers, or North and South Korea, shows how FOA's approach can engage with a large intellectual agenda.

Yet it can also work on a small scale. Two recently completed projects are restaurants for the Belgo chain in London and New York. A backland site off the fashionable Ladbroke Grove in London, the restaurant space is an amorphous form which defies categorisation as a volume, plane or strip: it is an environment where architecture and the experience of eating are contiguous and complementary.

Belgo Restaurants

Restaurants in New York and London show Foreign Office Architects' form-making ideas on a relatively small scale. Fluid and enticing, they achieve something of the qualities of the best public spaces: they also work commercially, using ramps and walkways to bring diners into deep, backland spaces.

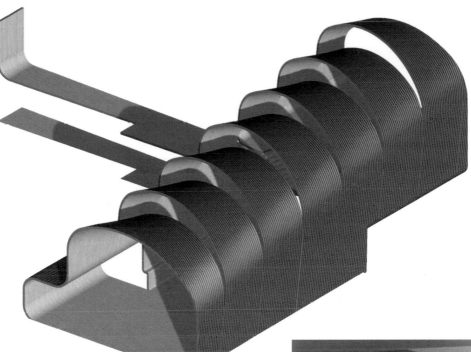

Belgo Zuid, London: ceiling and floor planes define a route from the street to the backland restaurant, where warped and folded hoops define and complex intriguing space.

Belgo New York: view from ramp down to lower level, upper level ceiling visible above.

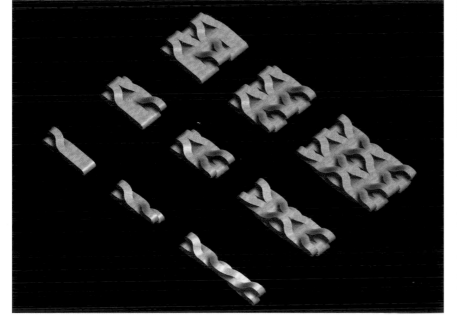

The Virtual House

An attempt to explore the virtual world in a domestic project: how folding and warping might create space and form without resorting to tradition or historical reference.

Yokohama International Port Terminal, Japan

An artifact which aims to be a physical and functional mediation between the system of passenger flow through a transport terminal, and the system of Yokohama's public spaces. Its warping and folded forms create a specific and highly intense experience of moving through it; the ground plane is at once an extension into the bay of the city's public space, but each opening offers a particular option – shopping, eating, meeting or embarkation. Here a complex architectural form is both flexible but also specific enough to differentiate routes and boundaries.

View of roof plaza

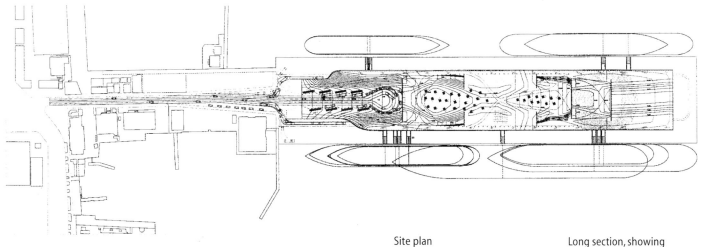

Site plan

Long section, showing deformation of ground plane.

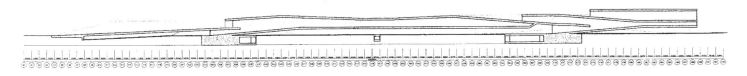

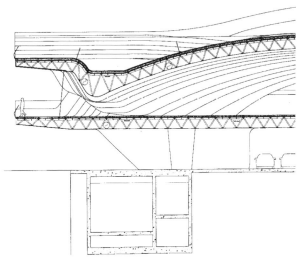

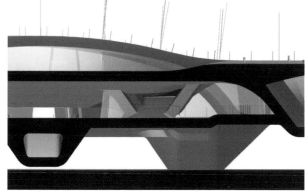

Cross section of restaurant and shopping zone: the traditional division between building structure and envelope disappears. Structural forces trace their paths as specific instances within a continuum rather than in pre-determined elements.

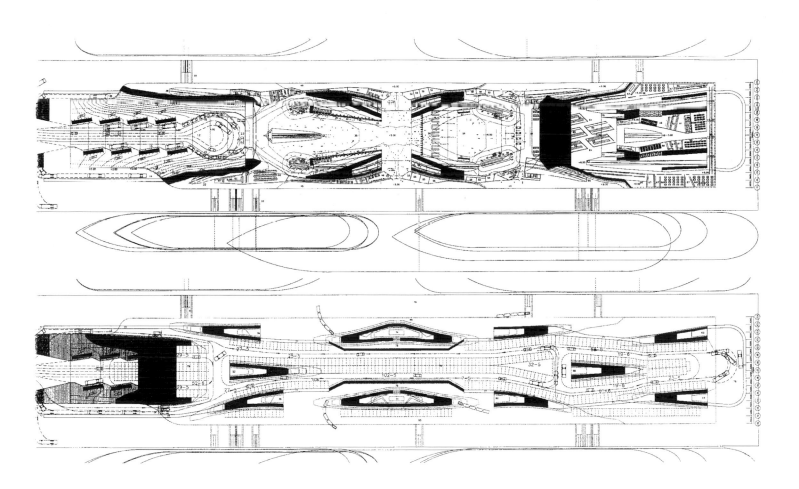

Ferry Terminal, Santa Cruz,
Tenerife

A competition entry for a new
ferry terminal with ambitions
to focus the city's public
spaces, several roads, in
particular re-establishing
waterfront access and drawing
together several roads which
radiate towards the city
centre.

The city lies between a
dramatic volcanic landscape
and the sea: the terminal
mediates between its order
and the forces of nature.

The varying levels create many
public spaces suitable for
different functions.

Site plan

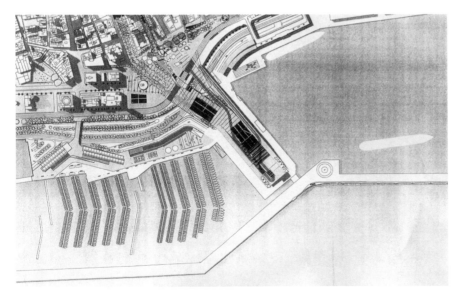

Myeong-Dong Cathedral
Precinct, Seoul, South Korea

In this competition entry,
Foreign Office Architects
proposed to enhance the
existing topography to create
an outdoor urban public space,
and a sunken covered stadium.
The manipulated and prolifer-
ated ground planes respect
the emotive religious and
political history of the area,
and its reality as a thriving
commercial district, but avoid
conventional typologies of
expression.

Aerial view of the precinct

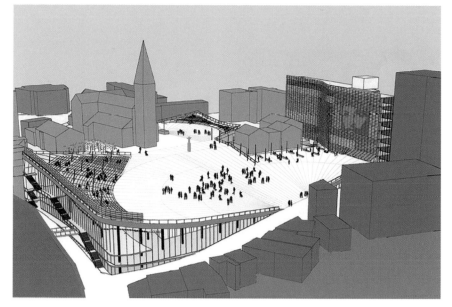

The proposal offers many
possiblities.

The stadium is a vast, entirely
new space.

Haworth Tompkins London

Haworth Tompkins's architectural agenda started to emerge through several projects from the second half of the 1990s. One is a small factory in rural Northamptonshire where Doctor Marten's boots are made, and two others are offices, in the off shore islands of Jersey and the Isle of Man. With fairly straightforward programmes, each gave an opportunity to develop specific architectural themes. At the Cobbs Lane factory it was using the form and scale of vernacular barns with a soft and sensuous local stone, combined with the precision and elegance of a crisply designed steel roof truss which minimises structures and maximises natural light. La Motte Street in Jersey and the Isle of Man building both show an ability to use a compositional language of steel and glass: in Jersey within a tightly gridded street pattern, on the Isle of Man for a long sea front promenade.

These projects show debt to their previous experience. Graham Haworth and Steve Tompkins both worked at Bennetts Associates, Haworth for Skidmore Owings and Merrill, and Tompkins for Arup Associates after leaving Bath University. All are places which match a strong formal language to a functional programme.

Recent projects show an ability to develop their architectural language for programmes which are either more complex or harder to define. A manor refurbishment of the Royal Court Theatre in London's Sloane Square – a dull 19th century theatre but one of a handful of venues which specialise in innovative, new drama often by young playwrights – achieves a remarkable synthesis. It respects the existing fabric, significantly improves the facilities, with an upgraded stage and a well equipped and flexible theatre studio in the attic, and provides a greatly expanded foyer under the road which leads directly into the square. The city's public realm and theatre's public space mingle with minimal division: the most obvious barrier is the red-painted wall to the auditorium.

Offering Shakespeare over the summer season, the Open Air Theatre in London's Regent's Park is more overtly populist and romantic. It is also very low cost and Haworth Tompkins's early proposals are essentially about manipulation of landscape and the objects within it, which could be seen as follies if their purpose were not apparent. Their most open-ended programme is for a building on the South Bank of the Thames in London: near to the Arts Centre, its client is an innovative housing association, and it will provide social, working and cultural facilities on the fourth side of a housing block.

Office buildings, Isle of Man
and Jersey

Haworth Tompkins's office
building on the Isle of Man
repeats the rhythm of the 19th
century seafront, but in a
modern language of white
walls, steel and glass.

The Jersey building matches
the rigour of its street grid in
its architecture, unlike its
neighbours.

Doctor Marten's Factory,
Northamptonshire

Additions to the factory
include two staggered wings
linked by a circulation spine.
An innovative roof structure is
designed to be minimal,
maximising natural light, while
the exterior form is similar to
the local vernacular barns, and
clad in a soft and warm local
stone to blend with its village
location.

View of interior

Section through new assembly
wings

Site plan: additions in black

Royal Court Theatre, London

A major redevelopment of an ordinary late 19th century theatre which has acquired a reputation for innovative new drama. It is located on London's Sloane Square, its site hemmed by an underground rail line and sewer. Planning restrictions preclude extra height, so expanding under the road was the only way of creating much needed extra foyer space; this also makes the square much more accessible to the public. The auditorium is improved and expressed as a red drum, stage facilities expanded, a new studio space added in the attic, and cor ten steel clad offices along the side alley.

The foyer is kept simple and plain, but seats and sightlines are improved.

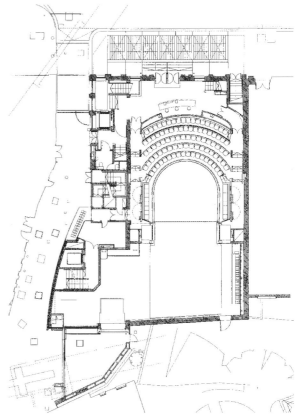

Plan at circle level

Section: the foyer is a space in itself, not just an entry to the theatre: the auditorium is clearly expressed.

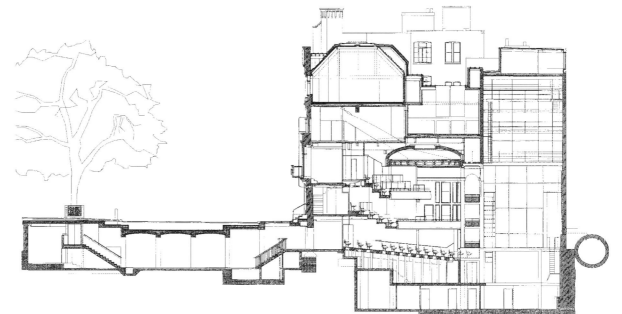

The dull neo-classical facade becomes a screen rather than a barrier.

New and old fabric is clearly distinguished.

Foyer. The red drum of the foyer is visible at the back: this forms the real distinction between open and enclosed space – the foyer is intermediate.

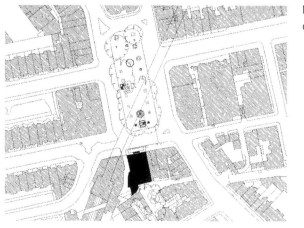

Site plan marking underground railway to the left of the theatre, sewer below and showing extent of the new foyer.

Views of the side alley on the Royal Court Theatre, where the metal-faced backstage facilities meet the existing brick flank wall.

Plan at foyer/stalls level

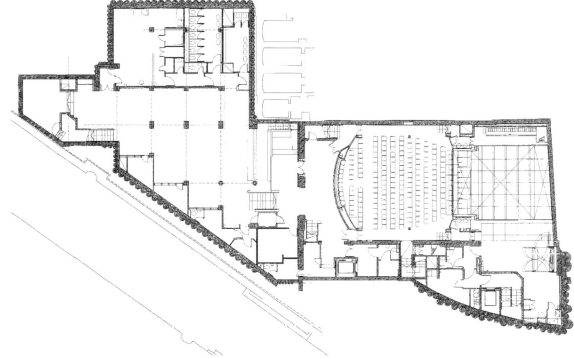

Open Air Theatre, Regent's
Park, London

A different site, repertory and
audience for this theatre
which runs during the summer. A very low budget calls
for ingenious solutions –
manipulating the landscape
and using trained plants as
much as possible.

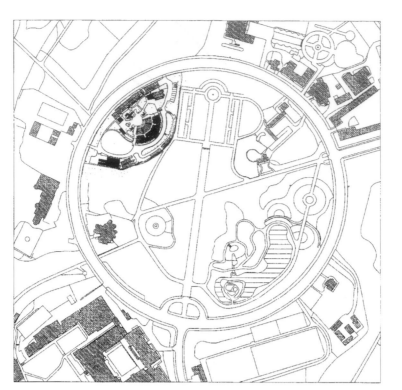

Ground level plan. Conventional structure is only used where
strictly necessary. The precinct
is screened by shaped hedges.

Site plan. The theatre lies in
Regent's Park's inner circle,
where John Nash planned a
series of large villas.

Coin Street development,
London

Coin Street Community
Builders have been responsible for some fine houses and
business unit developments
on the almost adjacent to the
South Bank Arts Centre in
London over the last few years.
Haworth Tompkins' project
creates a new courtyard with
housing around three sides
and a 'Hothouse' community
and arts centre (in its early
design stages) on the fourth.

Model of the housing

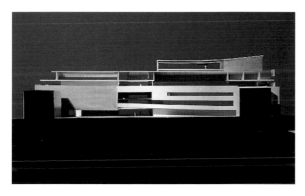

Model of the 'Hot house' and
site plan. Denys Lasdun's IBM
building lies between the site
and the River Thames.

Right: Ground floor plan, the
upper part is the 'Hot house'.

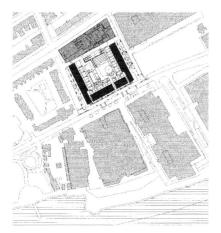

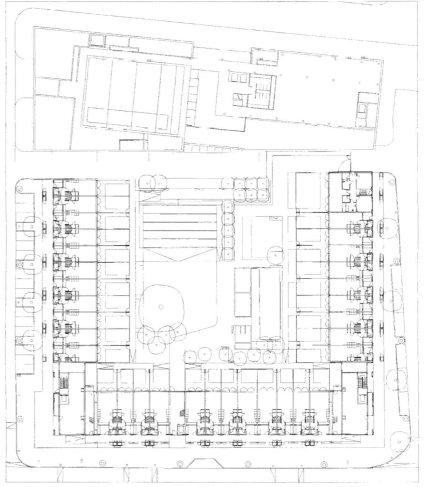

Stephen Hodder Manchester

Manchester-based Stephen Hodder had already begun to develop his own approach to a modernist formal language when he won the commission for a residential block for St Catherine's College, Oxford. Designed by the Danish architect Arne Jacobsen, it is one of the greatest buildings of the second half of the 20th century in Britain. Nikolaus Pevsner called it 'the perfect piece of architecture'. In the new wing Hodder's architecture acquired a rare refinement and sophistication, engaging both with the inward-looking existing building and the riverside condition of the site's perimeter. Its compositional language reflects Jacobsen's with a different palette of materials: large areas of glass and stainless steel sit within a concrete frame, their smoothness contrasting with the rough concrete, and all sitting on a plinth of the same brick as the original building. It accommodates 54 study bedrooms.

The Centenary Building for Salford University shows how the specific issues of a very particular formal language might have more general validity. Salford is an impoverished city within Greater Manchester, and its university is very different to Oxford's. Smaller budgets and a changing programme – the design started as a department of electrical engineering but it became an art and design school – give the robust detailing an extra edge: what is passive and serene at St Catherine's is active and didactic at Salford; stair details almost recall the window framing of Gropius's Bauhaus in Dessau. The narrow atrium which runs the length of the building is a space for overlooking and interaction, perhaps the only secure public space in the city.

In the Career Services Unit for Manchester University – a gentler environment – this language becomes more consciously a composition of volumes and planes. Lighting effects and the character of the interior space are crucial for what is essentially a small office building, another example of how Hodder manipulates a modern language to devise an internally consistent world.

New Residential Accommodation, St Catherine's College, Oxford

Arne Jacobsen's original college buildings, finished in 1964, attracted two criticisms: they would be impossible to extend, and they departed from the traditional college layout of rooms grouped around staircases. Stephen Hodder's building answers both: the 54 new study bedrooms and ancillary accommodation extend the college in an idiom which respects Jacobsen's masterpiece, adapting its language of form, material and detail to Oxford tradition. The horizontality of the original here is broken with vertical emphases – staircases around which the bedrooms are grouped.

Aerial view of St Catherine's College Oxford. The college lies on the edge of Oxford. Hodder's building lies to the right of the playing fields; Arne Jacobsen's the main college is above them. On the right can be seen the edge of the St Cross Library building by Sir Leslie Martin and Sir Colin St John Wilson, which houses the Bodleian (i.e. main university) Law Library, the English Faculty Library, and the Department of Statistics.

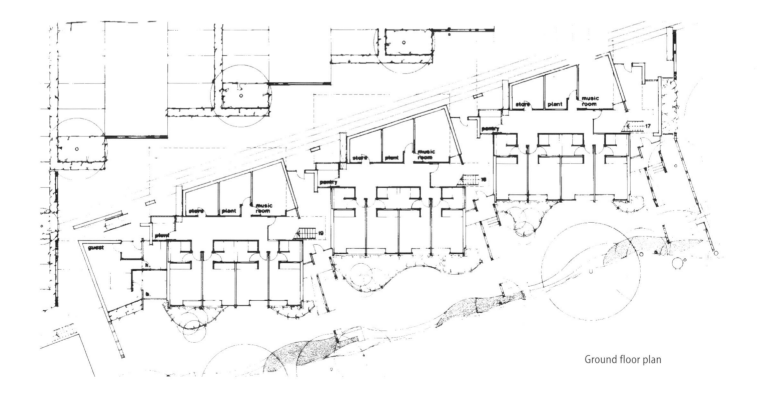

Ground floor plan

View from the south west

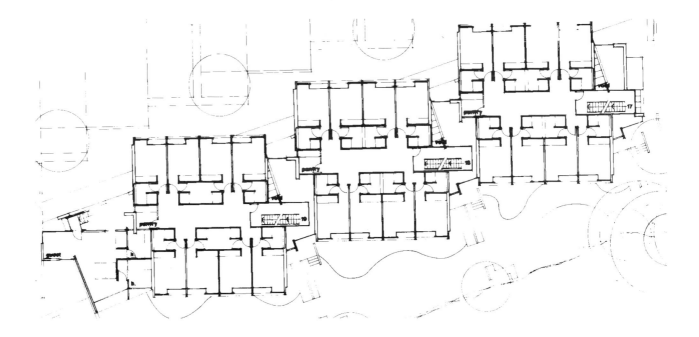

First floor plan

A concrete frame holds wall
panels and recessed windows.

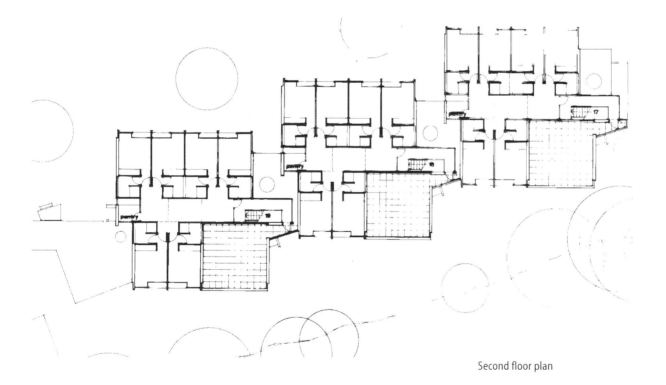

Second floor plan

Centenary Building,
Salford University

Another university building
which also uses a modernist
language, but here with no
context to support it. As a
faculty rather than residential
building, it focusses around a
long, thin atrium: seminar
rooms and lecture theatres
break free of the controlled
but animated composition.

The facetted curve houses
lecture and seminar rooms.

Site plan: Salford is terminal
point of the Manchester Ship
Canel. Once dominated by
busy wharfs and warehouses,
it has been left behind by
Manchester's renaissance. The
Centenary building forms an
edge to the campus.

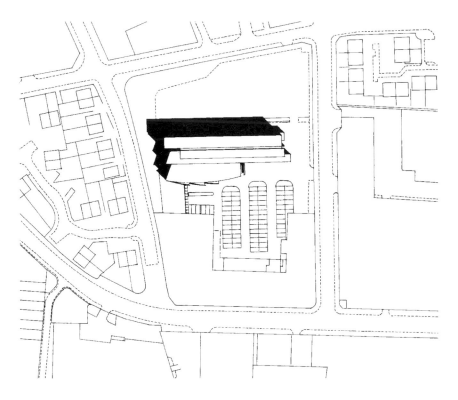

The Centenary Building attempts to bring an urban feel to its disparate campus, here trying to form one side of a courtyard.

Ground floor plan

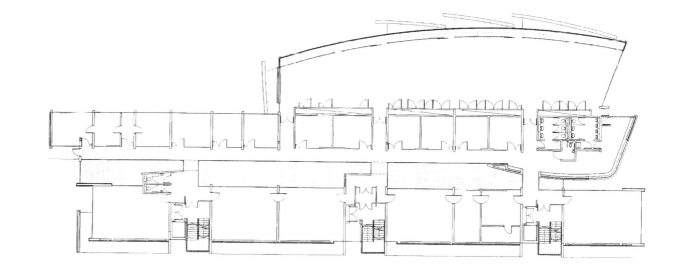

Career Services Unit,
Manchester University

The CSU is a semi-commercial
and autonomous unit within
the unversity; consequently it
operates from its own building, a composition whose
apparent abstraction belies its
fitness to purpose: helping to
make most effective use of
students' skills.

The east elevation may appear
to be an abstract Corbusian
composition, but its windows
and projections give character
to the interior spaces.

Site plan

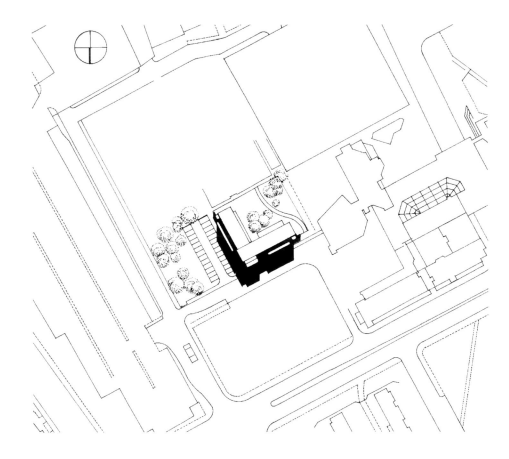

Career Services unit, ground
floor plan: the L-shape plan
creates an inner more intimate
court and an outer, tougher
face.

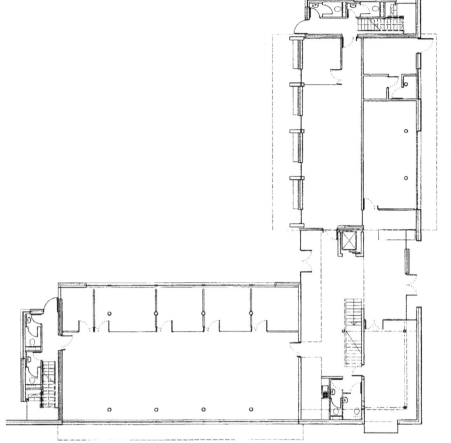

An early work, the Colne
Swimming Pool at Colne,
Lancashire, shows a less
refined language.

The City Road Surgery in a
tough part of Manchester
projects an order for one of
the area's few public buildings.

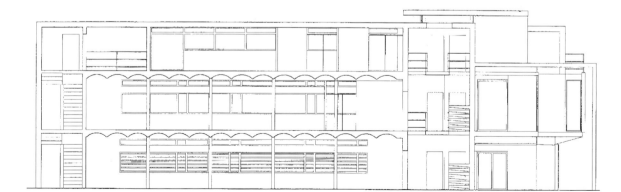

Career Services unit, section:
the barrel-vaulted ceilings,
careful attention to lighting
and creation of unexpected
views at points where the
volumes overlap relieves the
monotony of office work.

Niall McLaughlin London

Niall McLaughlin brings a highly original approach to form-making in his architecture. Coming from sources which are at once pragmatic, intuitive and intellectual, this gives his buildings a freshness and vitality, and the ability to conjure the unexpected effect. Paintings are often a stimulus; he devises built manifestations of the effects they depict, such as borrowing light from unexpected sources. In his re-working of a Carmelite monastery in central London, the sacristy expresses a rigour in the proportional system of the cupboards which contrasts with sunlight modulated through the roof: both the rationality of proportions and the power of light, to a Roman Catholic priest, denote the presence of God. Monastic tradition and the limits of the existing building were both factors which set parameters for the designs.

Two domestic projects, an apartment in a house in London's fashionable Notting Hill district, and a sizeable house in a South Kensington mews, show a similar ability to conjure unexpected spaces within constraints of existing buildings and sites. But they are more than exercises in maximising space; the spaces they make have a delicacy and subtlety which completely defies the given parameters. Careful placing of art works increases the sense of illusion and the visual intensity. These formal characteristics have a long history; they are not far from the techniques Sir John Soane used to transform his ordinary terraced house into a unique home and museum.

The photographer's shack, overlooking farmland in Northamptonshire, has a much freer form, which also derives from a combination of pragmatism and intuition. Here, however, budget rather than existing fabric provided the pragmatic constraints. Its construction process was almost mediaeval; its starting point was a model, and to save money there were no architectural drawings – the contractor was free to find his own way of building it to the outline of the model. It also fits sensuously between a low ridge between open farmland and a more formal garden. Opening its face to a small pond, it is both a passive element in the composition of the images its owner devises, and an active agent in helping to frame them. It is at the same time a retreat and a space for intense deliberation about nature.

Carmelite Monastery, London

Works to this complex include refurbishment of the sacristy, a private space where priests prepare to celebrate mass in the church, and the creation of a private chapel for the monks. Light and texture are the only available ornaments, and the work shows a fine degree of control of even the smallest details and objects.

Even the cupboards and drawers conform to a grand design.

The private chapel is converted from an existing room: careful treatment of surfaces and placement of furniture make it special.

Indicative section through the monastery sacristy, showing to the left: a contemplative seat with views over the garden, and the complex forming of the roof to create lighting effects.

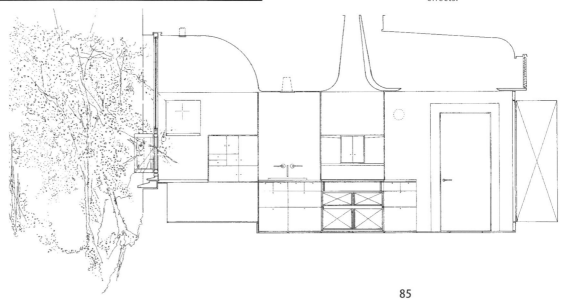

Apartment, Notting Hill,
London

An early project which sets out
an agenda of careful working
of space and surface within
the constraints of a standard
London terraced house.

View through the living room
to the balcony: Erno Goldfin-
ger's Trellick Tower in the
distance.

Section through staircase:
above is a roof-light, and the
carefully placed objects belie
physical limits.

House in Rutland Mews, South Kensington, London

Housing is often highly eccentric and personal, or extremely banal. This house is neither, despite the prosaic constraints of its site. Stepping the entrance facade creates a small forecourt and an outside wall which gives greater flexibility in planning; it also increases the opportunities to create effects. And even in a relatively small house a staircase can become almost processional in its movement from dark inner space to the light and open upper floor.

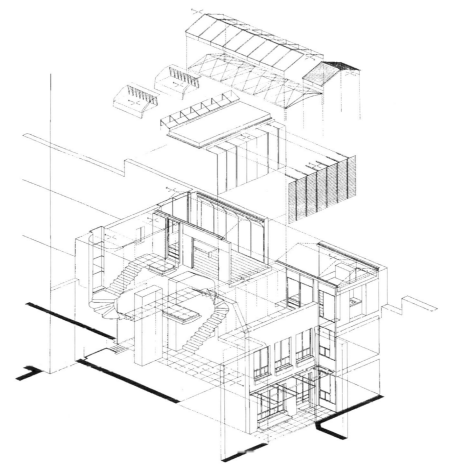

South (entrance) elevation

View from dining room towards staircase

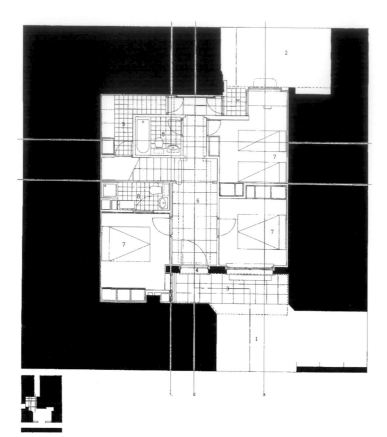

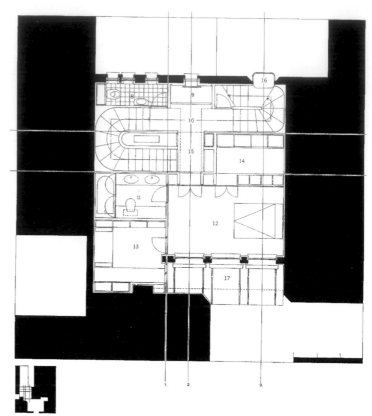

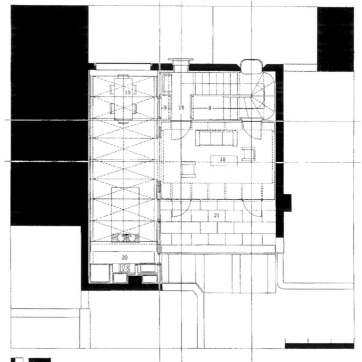

Ground floor plan

First floor plan

Second floor plan

1 Court yard
2 Garage lane
3 Glazed porch
4 Entry
5 Utility
6 Hallway
7 Bedroom
8 Bathroom/WC
9 Void
10 Landing
11 Master bathroom
12 Master bedroom
13 Master study
14 Master dressing room
15 Bridge
16 Tall window
17 Glass canopy
18 Living room
19 Dining room
20 Kitchen
21 Terrace

Section through staircase

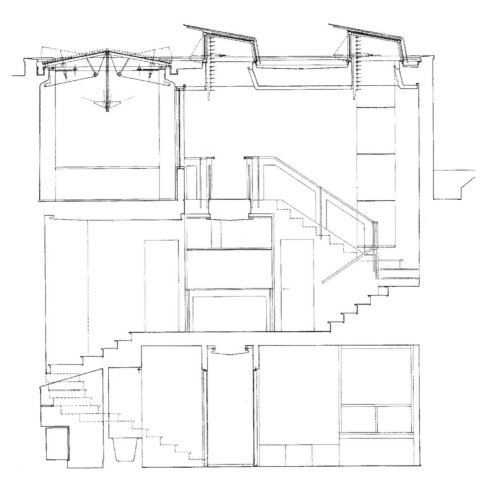

Photographer's Shack,
Northamptonshire

A extraordinary building: its
extravagant form belies its tiny
size. Yet its plan is beautifully
worked to construct as many
views as possible, to provide a
sauna and space for relaxation
and retreat. Its relationship to
its natural surroundings is
intimate and close, yet it is also
different: just as photography
differentiates between an
object and its image.

Detail of roof over pond

Site plan

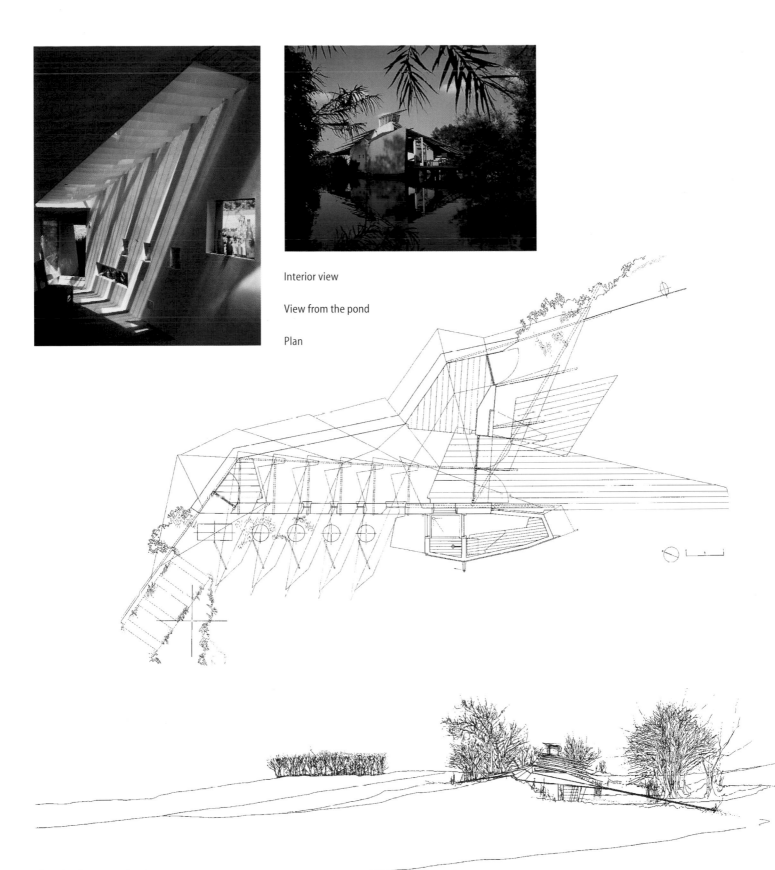

Interior view

View from the pond

Plan

Elevation from west: barely
visible from the farmland, it
opens to the pond.

Richard Murphy   Edinburgh

Richard Murphy, an English architect who has worked for most of his career in Scotland, has designed several projects which redefine the nature of institutions. This is a pressing concern as new institutions evolve in response to Scotland's move towards self government. Murphy's completed buildings are not yet on the scale or of the prominence of Enric Miralles's Parliament building in Edinburgh, but taken together they are at least equally significant as they both address the question of Scottish culture through their architecture and function, and are buildings which people are more likely to visit regularly.

His largest completed project is an arts centre in Dundee, a converted and extended warehouse in a former industrial city on Scotland's east coast whose prosperity declined along with the markets for its principale products, jam and jute for ropes. What indigenous culture the city has is largely textile-related, and the centre includes a gallery and workshop specifically for it. But it also brings art house cinemas and top lit gallery spaces capable of taking major travelling or specially curated exhibitions to the city: these are visible from either end of the main stairway which leads from the entrance to the bar area, the building's axial hub. Functionally, it blends culture and leisure, typologically, it develops themes which also emerge in the earlier Fruitmarket Gallery in Edinburgh, also a converted industrial building. In both the new roof is treated almost as a separate structure from the existing walls, folding an opening to create optimal lighting conditions.

A series of small, mainly residential projects were the laboratory for many of these concerns. Murphy devised a series of rooms which gently subverted Edinburgh's substantial domestic building stock: walls would turn into moving planes, corners open to the outside, and in one extreme case – as yet unbuilt – the two sides of a roof would tilt to open. Inside, the spaces are tightly and cleverly planned, often with carefully contrived views to enhance the sense of often small spaces. Also in clearly distinguishing new and old work, Murphy's architecture betrays his interest in Carlo Scarpa, about whom he has written and lectured.

The themes of cleverly worked domestic space and re-thinking institutions for contemporary circumstances come together in Maggie's Centre, a small charity where cancer sufferers can go for information and advice. Its design, in a converted stable, deliberately assumes a domestic character: spaces are small (although they can open to form a large space), it is well lit, and furnished more like a home than a hospital – a refuge of familiarity where the unknown and the feared might be contemplated.

Dundee City Arts Centre

A project about resolution and synthesis, between: old and new which grows out of it; the upper level of the city and the lower level of the old marshalling yards; culture and leisure; and between institutions, here the city council and the university. The junction of the two wings is a large bar and café, which looks up to the main entrance and out across the River Tay. On the same level are the two cinemas, and above are the public galleries. Much is made of tantalising glimpses between the different zones of the building, between inside and outside or just for natural light. Culture is not a series of discreet activities; they are connected to each other and the wider community.

A new institution within the city of Dundee

The centre sits on a sloping L shaped site with an entrance, bookshop (offices above), cinemas and grand staircase in one wing, and galleries in the other.

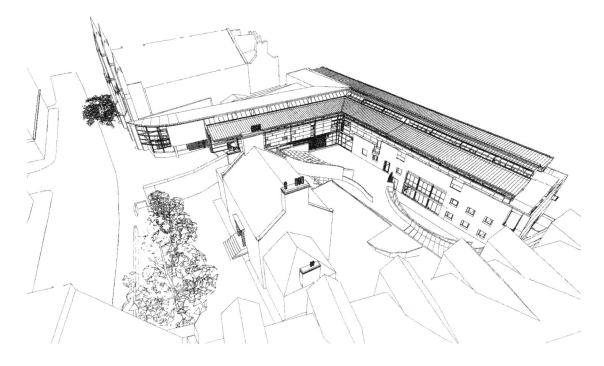

93

The foyer looking towards the galleries with stairs to the right and overlooked by offices to the left.

A cleverly formed roof lights the main gallery. Off it are small spaces for installations or looking out over the river.

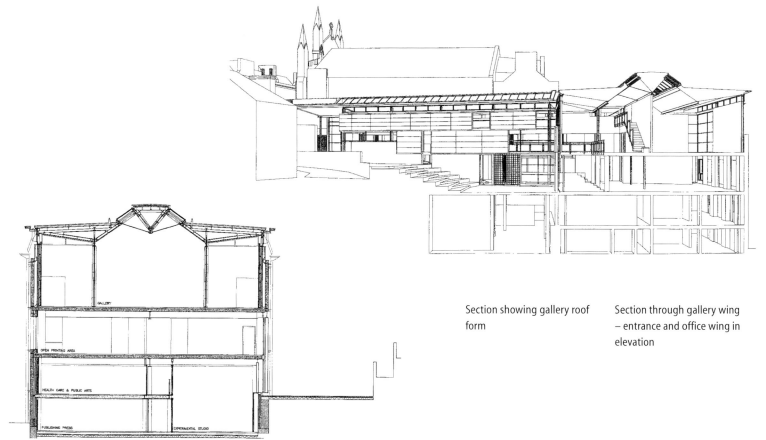

Section showing gallery roof form

Section through gallery wing – entrance and office wing in elevation

Fruitmarket Gallery, Edinburgh

Another former industrial building where fruit was raised from the low level railway track and raised to be stored or transferred to road. The restored stone facade shows traces of the new insertions, but they do not dominate. Inside a valley roof creates clerestory and central roof lights – the whole gallery is naturally lit.

Street view: a few modest signs denote the change of use from selling fruit to displaying art.

Exploded axonometric showing the composition of layers and components creating richly worked spaces.

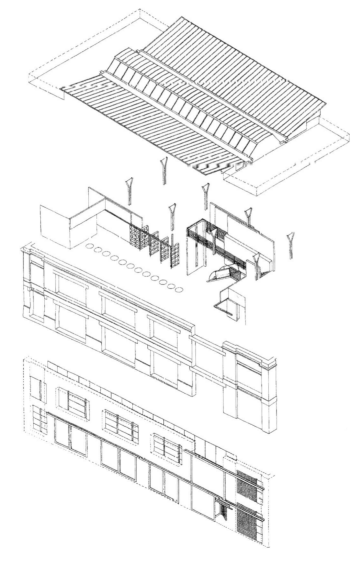

95

The gallery interior has an intimate feel.

Section

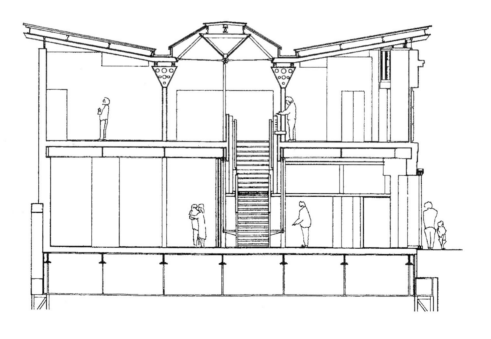

Maggie's Centre, Edinburgh

Former stables at Edinburgh's Western General Hospital are converted to give this innovative counselling centre for cancer victims an intimate and domestic air. This is achieved with careful light sources, comfortable, tactile materials and spaces which can be confined and private or overlooked and sociable.

Exterior detail. New insertions can be handled with sensitivity, as exemplified here.

The interior, a space for reassuring and reaffirmation

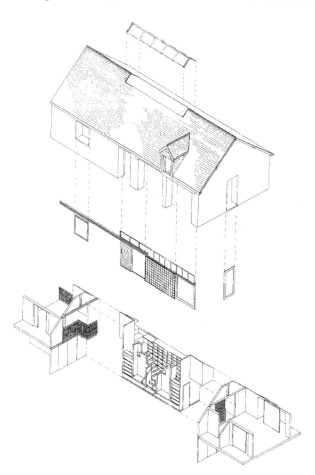

Exploded axonometric showing the delicate layering of new and old

North elevation. The small scale vernacular building dominates – the additions do not threaten or overwhelm.

House in Royal Terrace Mews,
Edinburgh

A small house converted from
former stables whose rough
construction invites almost
industrial treatment on the
facade, although its layering
reveals something of the
complex interior conjured
from a series of horizontal and
vertical planes.

Street elevation   Elevation study

Sections: the interior volumes
almost all interweave or
overlook each other. Mirrors
under the roof apex on each
wall enhance the apparent
space within a small house.

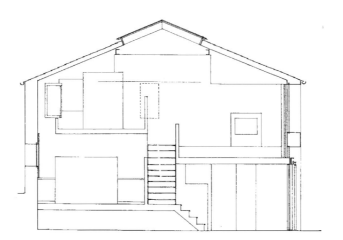

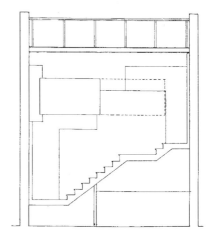

98

Proposed house off Royal Mile,
Edinburgh

Like Edinburgh itself, this
house opens up to reveal a
wealth of tantalising spaces
and relationships.

Roof open to admire distant
views.

Roof closed against the
weather.

Eric Parry London

Eric Parry's rich formal language started to emerge in several projects of the late 1980s. His compositions refer both to their own construction – there is an expressive clarity to how load is carried and a hierarchy of components – and to the forms and typologies of architectural tradition. They evoke both the pragmatic and immediate, and the intellectual, hidden and abstract. They also engage with the conditions of their sites, in climate, function and history.

In three recent projects, Foundress Court at Pembroke College Cambridge, an apartment building in Kuala Lumpur, Malaysia and a monumental spike at the south end of London Bridge it reaches its most sophisticated expression yet. Each is different. At Pembroke, one of Cambridge University's oldest colleges, the site has enormous historical resonance. The space between the new building and the edge of the site becomes a series of semi-hidden, almost magical areas through which the building differentiates its own intrinsic order from the outside world, an order which becomes apparent from the garden court where the beautifully worked facade speaks both of its masonry construction and suggests an order for the student rooms behind. Each room has a major and a minor window, and is equipped for concentrated comfort rather than idle luxury, the functional counterpart of the architectural expression in the facade.

Responding to the tropical climate of Malaysia, the Kuala Lumpur apartment block adds a notion of layering and depth to Pembroke's tightly planar composition. Allowing easy air movement is essential for comfort, so the design allows for many configurations of the different layers to suit varying needs for privacy and climatic conditions. As the units are much larger – up to 400 sqm – than the small student rooms at Cambridge, there is also more scope for spatial variety and the creation of spatial sequences, such as that from the street, through the entrance and across a walkway overlooking a swimming pool and garden.

The Southwark spike is an extraordinarily condensed form – a magnificent piece of masonry that stands up on an angle because it is held together with a steel rod. Yet it is passed by people 26 million times every year, and its character and appearance change with its context. Nearby, under a concrete walkway, is a bureau with tourist information about the area's attractions, including Shakespeare's Globe Theatre and the Tate Gallery of Modern Art – a richness which the spike's protean character implies.

Student Accommodation and Master's Lodge, Pembroke College Cambridge

Pembroke College's origins are 14th century. It has buildings by Christopher Wren and Alfred Waterhouse, as well as less distinguished architects, but its most striking characteristic is its series of delicately woven courts which have grown eastwards. Eric Parry's building defines one corner of the college where a suburban Master's Lodge had stood, and it continues the tradition of creating courts – a series of small ones mediate between it and the site's edge, and showing its most formal face inwards. The construction is as carefully worked as the plan, a compressed composition of trabeated stone frame and, slightly recessed, stone and window infill. The benefits of this careful working are apparent in the student rooms; each has two windows and provision to make studying enjoyable.

View from north

Student rooms provide for intellectual comfort rather than physical luxury.

Materials and details add intrigue to the staircase.

View from south along street: the short arcade offers a glimpse into the college world.

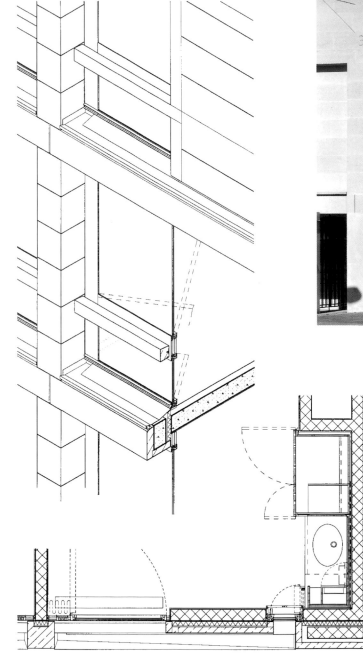

Isonometric and part plan of wall constuction

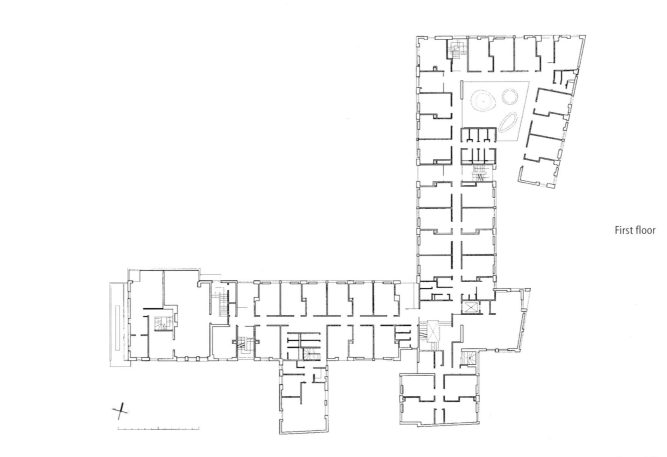

First floor

Ground floor plan

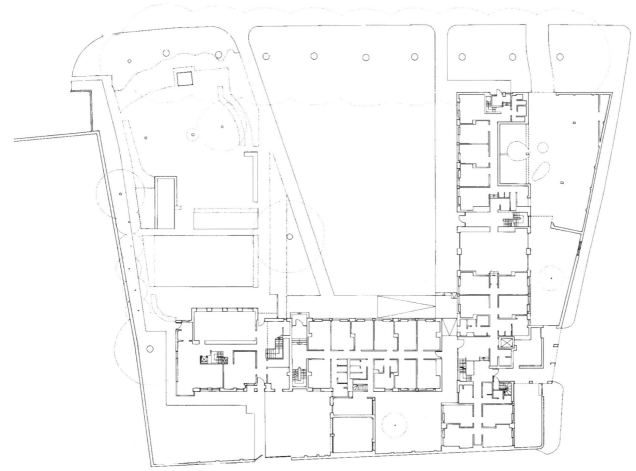

103

Damai Suria Apartment Block, Kuala Lumpur, Malaysia

Parry's design creates a series of volumes and planes which allow looseness for ventilation and screens for privacy within an overall order. What at Pembroke is compressed into tightly worked construction, here comes across in the interplay of volumes and planes – response as much to climate as to programme. Flats are grouped in clusters around shared spaces which lead into the development's garden and entrance, and thence to the street, creating a sequence of privacy which occupiers of luxury apartments might expect, but also recalling the elevations, whose layering of planes promises a richness of spatial expression.

View from the street: Petronas Towers in the distance

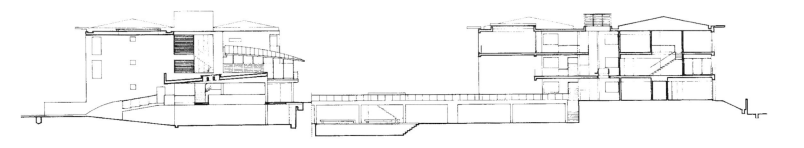

Section through the two blocks and garden

The entrance: a glimpse into a richly layered world

The garden facade: allowing for a variety of visual and climatic permeability to suit need and climate.

The garden at night, privacy with proximity

Axonometric

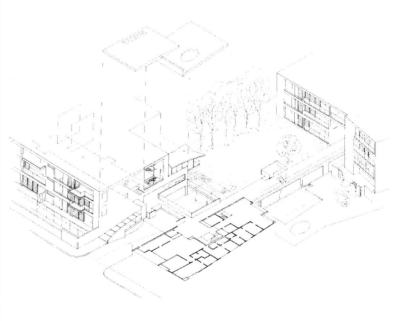

Southwark Visitors Centre and Monument, London

Southwark was London's first suburb and has always suffered from providing the services needed by the City of London across the river. Now it is cheap offices and transport. This two part project comprises a post tensioned, inclined stone spike – an ever changing and eye catching object which achieves an abstraction through wonderfully refined masonry, and a small centre with information about the area's history which occupies forgotten space beneath a concrete walkway.

Aerial view: rail tracks to London Bridge Station at bottom. London Bridge itself is to the top right.

Composite collage of the Southwark Gateway, showing the visitors centre and spike

106

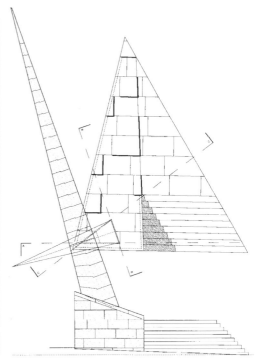

The spike occupies a wonderful territory between the specifics of its construction …

… and the abstraction of its form – which finds a use.

Setting out drawing for the Southwark Gateway

Interior of information centre

SHED KM Liverpool

Liverpool, the home city of the two practices which merged in 1997 to form Shed KM, poses specific and intense architectural challenges. It has a legacy of fine 18th and 19th century buildings – many built with the direct or indirect profits of the slave trade – and an unassailable position in the history of popular culture. Its recent past, though, is unfortunate; the docks declined, passenger shipping disappeared and the traditional industries of its neighbour and rival Manchester also suffered. In the 1980s Liverpool was characterised by the success of its football team while its left wing council pursued policies which appeared to be intended to flaunt opposition to the central government of Margaret Thatcher, rather than to regenerate the city.

At the end of the 1980s and early 1990s, King Mac Allister and Shed started to offer images of hope. Several projects for Liverpool University, including an extension to the school of architecture brought a crisp, high tech sensibility to the city, but they were in a relatively exclusive institution. By contrast the Baa Bar brought modern design and urban culture to a run down part of the city centre. Its success, buoyed by new sources of funding for urban regeneration, led to several projects in the same area, including the creation of Concert Square, an entirely new public space surrounded by bars, cafés and restaurants. The Ricci Bar connects Concert Square to Bolt Street, which has revived as a fashionable shopping street partly because of the increased volume and hours of trade which the Concert Square development brings.

All of this is achieved using a clear and crisp architectural language which derives from that part of modernism which allows for pragmatic handling of materials and forms. It generates light, movement and possibilities for display which match the populist and fashionable aims of the developments within the framework which the existing city fabric and infrastructure creates.

The Collegiate School and the Match Factory take this approach into a larger scale. In the former they have created 95 apartments by keeping the facade, the entrance hall and staircase in the grandiose 19th century Gothic building. The rhythm and scale of the facade delineates large, double height living spaces behind, which in turn suggest a plain modernist aesthetic. The Match Factory, in the Liverpool suburb of Garston, already has a remarkably modernist composition of frame and glass blocks despite dating from 1917. With minimal interventions for servicing the circulation, it is being converted into workshop units.

By subtly altering the economic constituents, Shed KM unite the social aims of providing housing and employment with the popular and consumerist cultural agenda of fun and fashion, within a modernist architectural language.

Concert Square and Ricci Bar,
Liverpool

Concert Square dates from
1995, when Shed and develop-
er Urban Splash created this
new urban space in a tightly
packed area of 19th century
warehouse buildings near
Liverpool's centre. The buildings had the usual mix of
occupations in a low-rent area,
and the new square and cafés
around it captured a public
mood. The latest addition to
the complex is the Ricci Bar,
which runs through an entire
block, connecting Concert
Square to Bold Street, an
established shopping area.
Architecture and urban space
here offer opportunities for a
mutually beneficial relationship between evening and
daytime activities, between
leisure and work.

View towards Concert Square:
opening to shop is visible on
the right.

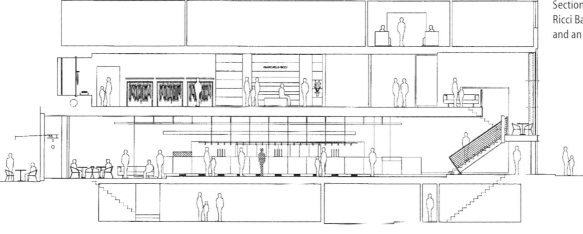

Section: Bold Street to left. The
Ricci Bar combines a café/bar
and an upmarket clothes store.

Concert Square view at night

Bar interior: assembly
of components

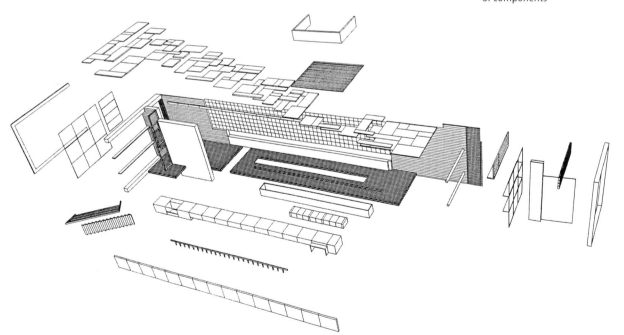

Staircase

View towards Bold Street

Collegiate School Regeneration, Liverpool

A grandiose building designed by Harvey Lonsdale Elmes (who also designed Liverpool's St George's Hall) in 1843, but which became increasingly run down as its surrounding declined. After closing as a school in 1986 it became derelict. Shed and Urban Splash are converting it into 96 apartments; the preserved facade establishes large volumes which are worked in a modern idiom, creating a market for a new type of housing in a depopulated city centre.

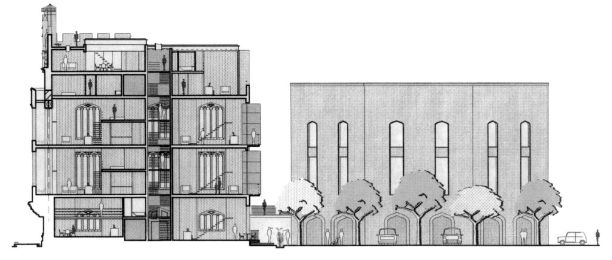

Section through preserved stair hall and formal garden

Section through corner flats: new windows are placed slightly inside the original oriel windows to create small balconies.

Typical flat plan: main level

Typical flat plan: mezzanine

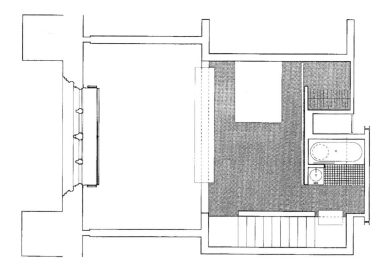
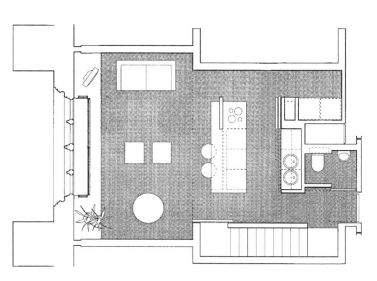

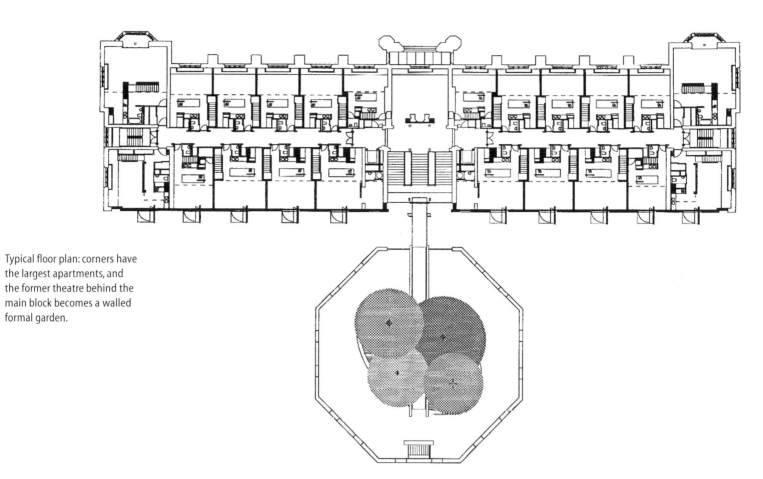

Typical floor plan: corners have the largest apartments, and the former theatre behind the main block becomes a walled formal garden.

Ongoing projects include the conversion of a 1917 Liverpool factory into business units: new additions include external stair towers.

Weston Williamson London

London Bridge Station, Weston Williamson's largest project to date, shows one line of development from the high tech architecture which dominated the British avant-garde in the 1980s. Both founder partners worked on seminal buildings of the period, Andrew Weston on the Richard Rogers Partnership's Lloyds headquarters and Chris Williamson on Michael Hopkins and Partners' Schlumberger research facility outside Cambridge; tented with a dramatic filigree structure, it remains the epitome of high tech as the idiom for object buildings on green field sites. Weston Williamson's early projects showed how a similar approach could be brought to converting buildings; rationally designed and assembled components could be inserted into existing spaces to transform their function and appearance.

London Bridge takes this to a different level. Here the rationality of high tech aesthetics explicitly engages with historic spaces. The station is a complex interchange of levels and transport systems which has evolved over 150 years with little co-ordination. It is one of the stops on the new Jubilee underground line extension, and Weston Williamson's commission covers new and refurbished tunnels and platforms, remodelling of the ticket hall and various entrances.

Here the kits of parts and assemblies of components, designed with the familiar high tech rationality, are used in an unfamiliar way, as they engage with the existing structure. The elements give an overall coherence to the diverse spaces; their precision is not just an end in itself, but also acts as a counterpart to the 19th century brick vaulting of the ticket hall and existing tunnels. They suggest an order and a coding for the spaces: the overhead services 'boom', for example, carries the lighting system, speakers for public address announcements, and indicates patterns of movement within the cavern-like spaces. Much is hidden underground, but occasional glimpses into ticket halls and protusions above ground give an indication from the public realm of what lies below.

London Bridge is an extreme example of an important generic challenge which British architects face: how to re-use and often convert existing infrastructure for contemporary needs. Several of Weston Williamson's recent projects touch on similar themes but on a smaller scale and lower in key – showing that the approach has a broad validity.

London Bridge Station
A massive and complex task, to refurbish the entire underground station, to add platforms and access tunnels for a new line, and to improve entrances from surrounding streets and the main line terminal. As in many transport projects, engineering meets architecture; here much of the engineering is 19th century infrastructure inserted into an older street pattern. Weston Williamson's additions are refined components, showing the legacy of 'high tech' but in greatly simplified form rather than some of its more baroque derivations. They bring meaning to the tunnels and adapt them for human use.

The service boom contrasts with brick vaults.

The boom carrying lighting and public address continues along the platforms.

Metal panels sit within the tunnels' structural ribs, leaving the construction visible. Most panels are blue cast iron, but white vitreous enamel is used for the existing platforms.

East entrances to the mainline
rail concourse: a 19th century
arcade meets 20th century
steel trusses; the complex
evolved in many phases.

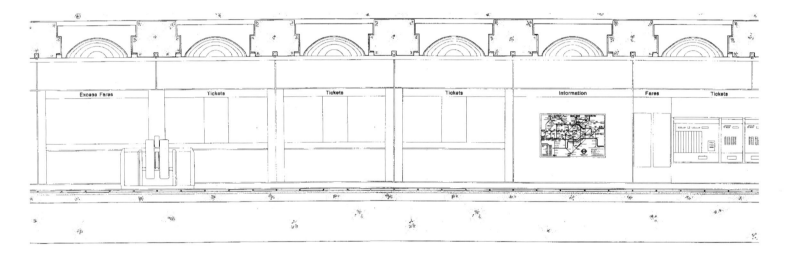

Section through a new ticket
hall under Borough High
Street.

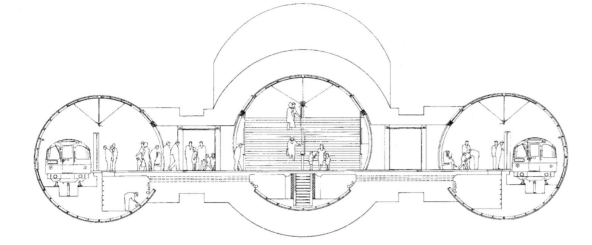

Section through the new
Jubilee Line

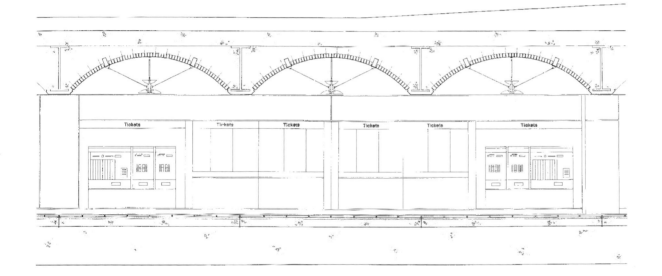

Section through a new ticket
hall under Borough High
Street.

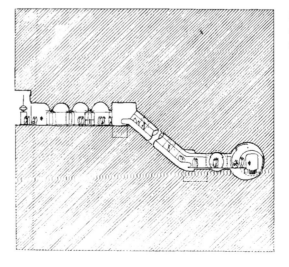

Diagram showing the different
conditions: ticket hall, escala-
tor, tunnel and platform.

117

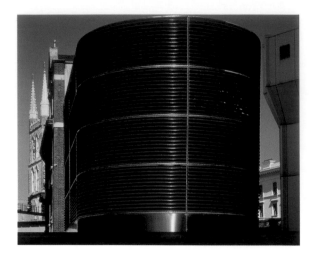

Ventilation shafts break through the surface and turn the internal surfaces of the underground into the external finish above.

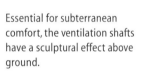

Essential for subterranean comfort, the ventilation shafts have a sculptural effect above ground.

New canopy at Putney Bridge
Station.

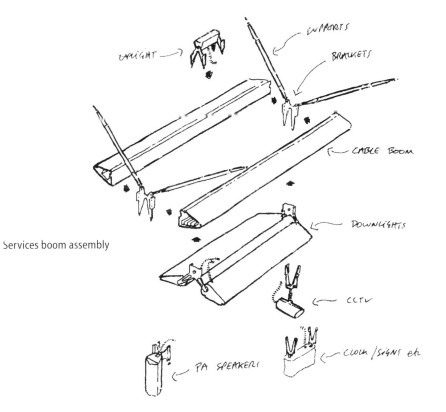

Services boom assembly

UPLIGHT

SUPPORTS

BRACKETS

CABLE BOOM

DOWNLIGHTS

CCTV

PA SPEAKERS

CLOCK / SIGNS etc

Weston Williamson's work for
London Transport includes
improving other stations and
maximising site values. Here:
Canopy study model.

Other projects develop the theme of a minimal high tech language, both to contrast with 19th century industrial settings, and to maximise a site's potential.
Tanner Street, South London, perspective view: close to London Bridge Station, this mixed use scheme includes a plot for Weston Williamson's own offices.

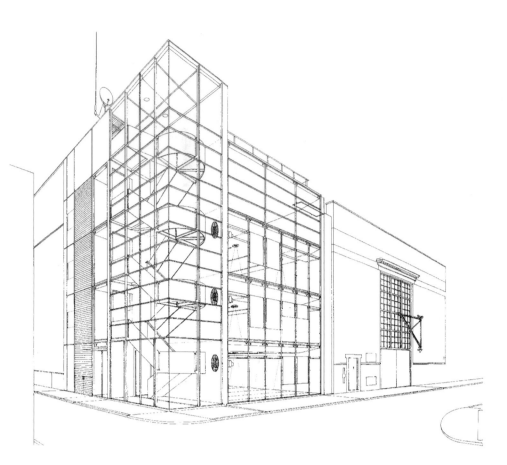

A retail warehouse in London's Docklands whose simplified design reflects in new materials is a modern reading of the basic construction of the original dock buildings. Perspective looking north.

National Energy Foundation
headquarters, Milton Keynes

A project which draws on a
mastery of the inherent nature
of materials and an understanding of how they can be
fashioned into functional
components, the NEF head-
quarters provides offices and
seminar/exhibition space, split
into a drum and a rectilinear
wing. With a very limited
budget, Weston Williamson
had to pare every part down
to a minimum and devise the
most efficient forms and ways
of using materials possible. It
also has to have low energy
consumption. The design
balances these two factors
ingeniously: a concrete frame
provides thermal mass and
cooling for the ground floor,
but could not be afforded for
the upper floor, which instead
uses a lightweight steel frame
with drylining for insulation.
Facades are also designed to
minimise solar gain and heat
loss, and to allow as much
daylight to penetrate as
possible.

The facades are contrived to
allow as much light in as
possible, while avoiding undue
heat loss or overheating.

The drum contains exhibition
and seminar space and the
wing houses offices; the
orientation and roofscape
makes provision for adding
photo-voltaic cells when funds
are available.

ALLFORD HALL MONAGHAN MORRIS

Block B, Morelands
5-23 Old Street
London EC1V 9HL
Founded 1989

Principals

Simon Allford, born 1961
Studied: Sheffield University and the Bartlett School
University College of London
Qualifications: BA Arch(Hons) DipArch

Jonathan Hall, born 1960
Studied: Bristol University and the Bartlett School,
University College London
Qualifications: BA Arch(Hons) DipArch MSc

Paul Monaghan, born 1962
Studied: Sheffield University and the Bartlett School,
University College London
Qualifications: BAArch(Hons) DipArch

Peter Morris, born 1962
Studied: Bristol University and the Bartlett School,
University College London
Qualifications BA(Arch) (Hons) DipArch

Projects include
Walsall Bus Station, Walsall 2000
Work/Learn Zone, Millennium Dome, London 1999
CASPAR Apartments, Birmingham 1999
Great Notley School, Essex 1999
Peabody Apartments, London 1999

Our Lady of the Rosary School, Staines 1999
Morelands Buildings, London 1999
Millennium Products Touring Exhibition 1999
Broadgate Club West, London 1997
Portsmouth Players, Portsmouth 1997
North Croydon Medical Centre, Croydon 1997
Mica House, London 1996
Mallett House, London 1995
St Mary's School, London 1994
Glass House (project) 1994
Poolhouse, Wiltshire 1993
Melvin House, London 1992
Otoman Housing, Fukuoka, Japan (competition entry) 1990

Awards
RIBA Award 1995 – Poolhouse, Wiltshire
RIBA Award 1998 – Broadgate Club West
RIBA Award 1999 – North Croydon Medical Centre

BAUMAN LYONS ARCHITECTS

15 Hawthorn Road
Leeds LS7 4PH
Founded 1992

Partners
Irena Bauman and Maurice Lyons

Irena Bauman, born 1955
Studied: Liverpool University
Qualifications: BA(Hons) in Architecture, BArch(Hons)
RIBA MAPM

Maurice Lyons, born 1955
Studied: Liverpool University
Qualifications: BA(Hons) in Architecture, BArch(Hons)
RIBA Qualified Planning Supervisor

Simon Warren, born 1964
Studied: Birmingham School of Architecture
Qualifications: BA(Hons) Arch, DipArch
1st prize – RIBA Landscape and Design Initiative
Competition (with Mark Way)

Michael Trigg
Studied: Manchester Metropolitan University and
Nottingham University
Qualifications: BA(Hons) in Architecture 1st Class
(RIBA Part I)
Post Graduate Diploma in Architecture (RIBA Part II)

James Grogan
Studied: Hull School of Architecture
Qualifications: BA(Hons) Architecture, Barch with
commendation for design.

Neil Verow, born 1956
Studied: University of Nottingham
Qualifications: BA(Hons) in Architecture and Environ-
mental Design

Sheila Overton, born 1961
Studied: Oxford Polytechnic
Qualifications: BA(Hons) in Architectural Studies

Projects include
Bawn Avenue – new build office block, ongoing
Unity Housing Association Offices, ongoing
74 Kirkage – refurbishment of 60s office building,
ongoing
Leeds Media Centre March 2001
Yorkshire Sculpture Park, 2001
Public space with performance area in collaboration
with Pat Gilbey (writer) and Amy Edwars, (graphic
designer), Garston, Liverpool 2000
Bridlington Harbour 2000
Ferensway Development, Hull (competition entry)
1999
31 The Calls – refurbishment and conversion of
warehouse, Leeds, 1999
Young People's Cultural Centre, Liverpool, feasibility
study, 1999

ReVisions Exhibition, National Museum of Photo-
graphy, Bradford 1999
The Wardrobe – St Peters Buildings, Leeds 1999
Dry Dock Pub, Leeds 1998
Photo 98 projection installation in an underpass in
Bradford in collaboration with photographer Joachim
Schmidt, 1998
17/19 Wharf Street – warehouse conversion into
offices, Leeds 1998
Clifton Park Museum, The Rockingham Collection,
Rotherham 1998
Sheffield Cultural Industries Quarter, 1997
Northern School of Contemporary Dance, Leeds 1997
Shears Yard – warehouse conversion into offices and
restaurant, Leeds, 1997
Clarence Dock Bar, Leeds, 1997
Chinese Community Centre in collaboration with
artist, Madeleine Miller, Leeds 1997
Bridlington South Promenade in collaboration with
artists Bruce McLean and Chris Tipping and Susan
Hardistry (project architect), 1997

Awards include
RSA Art for Architecture Award 1997
Leeds Architecture Award for Sheltered Housing
Scheme 1996

BIRDS PORTCHMOUTH RUSSUM ARCHITECTS

8 New North Place
London EC2A 4JA
Founded 1989

Partners
Andrew Birds, born 1960
Studied: Leeds Polytechnic School of Architecture
Qualifications: BA Arch Dip Arch

Richard Portchmouth, born 1956
Studied: Kingston Polytechnic School of Architecture
Qualifications: BA(Hons) Arch Dipl Arch RIBA Part III

Mike Russum, born 1956
Studied: Kingston Polytechnic School of Architecture
Qualifications: BA(Hons) Arch Dipl Arch RIBA Part III

Projects include
Somerset House River Terrace Restaurant 1998
Oxford Street Christmas lights, London 1997
Imperial War Museum for the North, Manchester 1997
Laganside cross harbour development area, Belfast 1995
A13 Architectural and Artistic proposals 1995
Culture-Drome, Fairfield car park, England 1995
Croydon, Vision for the Future, England 1994
The British Museum inner courtyard, London 1994
Crossrail Station, Rickmansworth, England 1992
Stonehenge Visitors Centre, England 1992

Morecambe sea front, England 1991
Avenue de Chartres Carpark, Chichester, England 1991
122/124 Haberdasher Street, England 1987

Awards
Avenue de Chartres Car Park, Chichester, 1991/2
Civic Trust Award
RIBA Regional Award
Downland Design Award
West Sussex County Council Design Award
English Tourist Board Commendation

CARUSO ST JOHN ARCHITECTS

1-3 Coate Street
London E2 9AG
Founded 1990

Principals
Adam Caruso and Peter StJohn

Adam Caruso, born 1962
Studied: McGill University, Canada
Qualifications: BSc(Arch) BArch – McGill University

Peter StJohn, born 1959
Studied: Bartlett School, University College London, Architectural Association
Qualifications: BSc(UCL), AADip(Hons) Architectural Association

Projects include
Nara Convention Hall, Japan (competition, special prize)
Museum of Scotland, Edinburgh (competition)
Pleasant Place Surgery, Surrey

1992
East Midlands Arts Board Headquarters, Loughborough (competition)
Karlsruhe Bundesgartenschau 2001 (competition)
Private Residence, Isle of Wight

1993 –
Interior for Ove Arup Partnership, London
Studio House, London

Schlossgarten, Berlin (competition in collaboration with David Chipperfield)
Foyer, Birmingham (competition, finalist)

1994
Private Residence, Lincolnshire
House design for New British Architecture Exhibition, Architecture Foundation
Birkbeck College Management Centre (first stage shortlist)

1995
Stratford Advice Arcade, East London
Yokohama International Port Terminal competition, (honourable mention)
Limmo Peninsula Ecocentre (competition, finalist)
Private Residence, Kent
Social Housing, Frankfurt (competition)

1996
Walsall Art Gallery and Public Square (competition, first prize, under construction)
Highgate and Walsall Brewery New Public House, Walsall
Studio Hose, East London
Millennium Bridge, London (competition)
Furniture Stands for SCP Furniture, Cologne and Milan

1997
Warehouse Refurbishment, Clerkenwell
Rhapsodies in Black, Exhibition Design, Hayward Gallery, London
Flat in Mansion Block, London (construction in 2000)
The Photographers Gallery, London (competition finalist)

Greenwich Millennium Village (competition finalist)
Jyväskylä Music and Arts Centre, Finland (competition third prize)

1998
Mews House, London
Museum der Moderne, Auf dem Mönchsberg, Salzburg (competition)
Vertigo, exhibition design, Glasgow
Fruitmarket Bankside Directional Signage System, London Borough of Southwark (competition, first prize, under construction)
Furniture Stand for SCP Furniture, Cologne
Bundesschulzentrum Wörgl, Austria (competition, second prize)
Altenpflegeheim Oberndorf, Austria (competition)

1999
Warehouse Refurbishment, Clerkenwell (under construction)
Centre for Contemporary Arts, Rome (invited competition)
Hypocaust Museum, St Albans (invited competition)
Furniture Stand for SCP Furniture, Milan
Factory Refurbishment, Hackney (in production)
Public Square, Kalmar, Sweden (invited competition)

PATRICK DAVIES ARCHITECTS
8 Dorset Square
London NW1 6PU
Founded 1986

Patrick Davies, born 1957
Studied: Cambridge University School of Architecture,
Harvard University Graduate School of Design, and
British School at Rome.
Qualifications: MA and Dip Arch

Projects include
St David's Hotel, Cardiff, 1999
Advertising structures for Mills and Allen on various
sites, London 1994 onwards
Manchester Airport Hotel (project) 1994
Old Street Roundabout advertising structure, London,
1994
ECME factory, Oporto, Portugal (project) 1993
Offices in Old Street, London, 1991
Agincourt Road business units, London, 1990

FAT (Fashion Architecture Taste)
Appletree Cottage
116-120 Golden Lane
London EC1Y 0TL
Founded 1991, by Sean Griffiths, Kevin Rhowbotham
and Clive Sall

Sean Griffiths, born 1966
Founder member of FAT 1991
Studied: Manchester Polytechnic and Polytechnic of
Central London
Qualifications: BA Dip Arch

Sam Jacob, born 1970
Joined FAT 1995
Studied: at the Mackintosh School of Art, Glasgow,
and the Bartlett School, University College London
Qualifications: B Arch Dip Arch

Emma Davies, born 1968
Joined FAT 1995
Studied: Fine art at Chelsea School of Art, London
Qualifications: MA (fine art)

Charles Holland, born 1969
Joined FAT 1997
Studied: Polytechnic of Central London and the
Bartlett School, University College London
Qualifications: BA Dip Arch

Projects include
Conversion of Thomas Neal's Shopping Centre,
London (ongoing)
New house and office, London (ongoing)
Sitooterie, pavilion for at Belsay Hall, Northumber-
land, 2000
Shopping: exhibition of 30 contemporary artists'
prints on carrier bags, London (1999)
Carnaby Art Billboard, Carnaby Street London (1999)
King's Cross Millennium Artwork, four large scale
installations in King's Cross Station, London (1999)
Mambo Retail Environments, London, Manchester
and Brighton, 1999
Conversion of church into offices for Kessels Kramer
advertising agency, Amsterdam, 1998
Offices for Legas Shafron Davies advertising agency,
London, 1998
Institute of Contemporary Arts, new bar, café, front
of house and IT centre, London, 1997
Set design for MTV snowboarding awards, 1997
The Chez Garcon, conversion of chapel into house,
London, 1996
Outpost Venice Biennale, collectable exhibition at
the Venice Biennale, 1995
The Brunel Rooms nightclub, Swindon, 1995
Leisure Lounge nightclub, London, 1994
Adsite, exhibition of 200 artworks in bus shelters
around London, 1993

Awards
Shortlisted for Sutton Walk gateway to South Bank
competition, 1999
Shortlisted for Jane Drew prize for architecture, 1998
Shortlisted for Concept House competition, 1998

FOREIGN OFFICE ARCHITECTS LTD

58 Belgrave Road
London SW1V 2BP
Founded 1992

Principals
Farshid Moussavi and Alejandro Zaera Polo

Farshid Moussavi, born 1965
Studied: Bartlett School, University College London
and Harvard University Graduate School of Design
Qualifications: Dip Arch, BSc Architecture (UCL),
Masters in Architecture (Harvard)

Alejandro Zaera Polo, born 1963
Studied: ETS of Architecture, Madrid, Spain, Harvard
University Graduate School of Design
Qualifications: Diploma in Architecture Degree (Hons)
(ETS of Architecture in Madrid), Spain; Master in
Architecture with Distinction (The Graduate School of
Design, Harvard University)

Projects include
Yokohama International Ferry Terminal, Japan
completion March 2002
Belgo Restaurant, London 1999
Belgo Restaurant, New York 1998
Bermondsey Antiques Market Design, London 1997
Rome Congress Centre, Italy 1998
Redevelopment of Link Quay waterfront, Canary
Islands 1998
Pusan High Speed Railway Complex, Korea 1996
Kansai-Kan National Diet Library, Japan 1996
Myeong-Dong Cathedral of Seoul, Korea 1996
National Glass Centre, Newcastle, UK 1994

HAWORTH TOMPKINS ARCHITECTS

19/20 Great Sutton Street
London EC1V 0DN
Founded 1991

Principals
Graham Haworth and Steve Tompkins

Graham Howarth, born 1960
Studied: Cambridge University School of Architecture
Qualifications: BA, DipArch, Cantab RIBA
Graduated from Cambridge University with distinc-
tion in 1984

Steve Tompkins, born 1959
Studied: Bath University
Qualifications: BSc, BArch RIBA
Graduated from Bath University with a double first in
1983, winning the RIBA Silver Medal and an EEC
housing prize.

Projects include
Doc Martens Headquarters, Northamptonshire 1996
La Motte Street, Jersey 1996
Isle of Man – Phase 1 1998
Notting Hill House, London 1997
Royal Court Theatre, London 1999
Coin Street, London 2000

Awards include
RIBA Regional Design Award 1996. Cobbs Lane
Structural Steel Design Award 1996: Cobbs Lane
States of Jersey Major Building of the Year Award
1998: La Motte Street, Jersey

HODDER ASSOCIATES
Commercial Wharf
6 Commercial Street
Manchester M15 4PZ
Founded 1992

Principal
Stephen Hodder, born 1956

Studied: School of Architecture, University of Manchester – Selected as one of six architects to represent the emerging generation of British Architects in an exhibition at the Architectural Institute of Japan in Tokyo in October 1994 and has recently exhibited at the Biennale at San Paulo in Brazil. Awarded the Member of the British Empire

Projects include

1991
Swimming Pool, Colne, Lancashire
Castlegate Offices, Bury, Lancashire

1992
School of Business and Management, University College, Salford

1993
Apartments, Lytham St Annes, Lancashire
Oswald Medical Practice, Chorlton, Manchester

1994
Residential accommodation, St Catherine's College, Oxford
Goodwin Sports Centre, University of Sheffield

1995
Junior Common Room refurbishment, St Catherine's College Oxford
Extension to Manchester City Art Gallery, Manchester
Exhibition Design, British Art Show 4, Manchester
Visitor Centre, Jodrell Bank, Cheshire (competition entry)
Orientation Centre, Heaton Hall, Manchester, (competition entry)

1996
City Road Surgery, Hulm, Manchester
Centennary Building, University of Salford

1997
Masterplan for new campus, University of Nottingham (competition entry)
Masterplan for Coventry city Centre (competition entry)

1998
Golf Club House, Legh Park, Cheshire
Clissold Sports Centre, London
CUBE Gallery, Manchester
Levenshulme Health Centre, Manchester
Capenway Diving Centre, Cumbria
Swimming Pool, Walsall
National Wildlflower Centre, Knowsley, Liverpool
Sports Centre, Grange over Sands, Cumbria
Corporation Street Footbridge, Manchester

Awards include
Royal Fine Art Commission/Sunday Times Building of the Year Award 1991: Colne Swimming Pool in Lancashire
Grand Prize Royal Academy Summer Exhibition 1995: panels presented as part of the submission for the Manchester City Art Gallery competition
RIBA/Sunday Times Building of the Year Award 1996: Centenary Building, University of Salford

NIALL MCLAUGHLIN ARRCHITECTS
166 Portobello Road
London W11 2EB
Founded 1990

Niall McLaughlin, born 1962
Studied: University College Dublin School of Architecture
Qualifications: BA and B Arch

Projects include
Jacob's Ladder, private house, Oxfordshire, 1999
Extension to the De La Warr Pavilion, Bexhill (originally designed by Eric Mendelsohn and Serge Chermayeff) 1999
Housing development, Kensington, London, 1998-9
Ben Uri Art Gallery, Camden, London, 1997
Carmelite Monastery, new chapel and refurbishment, Kensington London, 1991-7
Photographer's Shack, Northamptonshire, 1996
Phillimore Club, swimming pool and health club, London, 1996

Awards
Young British Architect of the Year, 1998
British Representative, Sao Paolo Architecture Biennale, 1997
Royal Institute of Architects of Ireland regional awards for the Photographer's Shack (1999), Phillimore Health Club (1997), Carmelite Monastery (1996)

RICHARD MURPHY ARCHITECTS
34 Blair Street
Edinburgh
Founded 1991

Principal Richard Murphy, born 1955

Studied: Universities of Newcastle and Edinburgh
Qualifications: BA(Hons), DipArch, FRSA, ARIAS, ARSA, RIBA

Projects include
Centre for Contemporary Art & The Natural World, Exeter, ongoing

Housing Development at Cowgate, Edinburgh, ongoing
New Arts/Theatre Centre, Peebles, ongoing
Stirling Tollbooth Theatre (competition win) 2001
Napier University Computer Centre, Edinburgh 2001
Maggie's Centre, Cancer Caring Centre Phase II, Edinburgh 2000
Cottage at Buchlyvie, 2000
St Andrews University, Faculty of Divinity Residences, ongoing
New House, Broomhill, East Lothian 1999
Housing Project – Tron Square, Edinburgh (competition win) 2000
Learning Centre for East Dunbartonshire Council, 2000
Flat Development, Graham Square, Glasgow 1999

Competition winning project for a Contemporary Art Gallery, Dundee 1999
Harmeny School, Balerno 1999
Major extension, Barns House, Peebles 1999
Competition winning housing project for Edinburgh Development and Investment, Dublin Street, Edinburgh 1994
Renovation of Fruitmarket Gallery, Edinburgh 1993

Awards include
RIBA Award 1992: 29 Inverleith Gardens, Edinburgh
RIBA Award 1993: Fruitmarket Galley, Edinburgh
RIBA Award 1995: 49 Gilmour Road, Edinburgh
RIBA Award 1996: 17 Royal Terrace Mews, Edinburgh
RIBA Award 1997: Cancer Caring Centre, Edinburgh
RIBA Award 1998: 7 Abbotsford Park, Edinburgh
RIAI Award 1999: House in Galway

ERIC PARRY ARCHITECTS
87-89 Saffron Hill
London EC1N 8QB
Founded 1983

Principal Eric Parry, born 1952

Studied: University of Newcastle upon Tyne, Royal College of Art, Architectural Association
Qualifications: MA(RCA) MA(Cantab) AA Dip RIBA

Projects include
Pembroke College, Cambridge
Southwark Gateway, London
W3 Building, Stockley Park, London
Apartment Building, Kuala Lumpur, Malaysia
Ministry of Sound, London
Studios for the artists Tom Phillips and Antony Gormley, London
Sussex Innovation Centre, East Sussex
Granta Park, South Cambridgeshire
Lipton House, London
Chateau de Paulin, France
Taylor House, London

Awards
RIBA Regional Award, 1998 – Pembroke College

SHED KM ARCHITECTS

The Tea Factory
92 Wood Street
Liverpool L1 4DQ
Founded 1997 (from the merger of Shed and King MacAllister)

Jonathan Falkingham, Founding Member, born 1963
Studied: Liverpool University
Qualifications: BA Barch RIBA

Dominic Wilkinson, Director, born 1965
Studied: Liverpool University
Qualifications: BA Barch MA RIBA

Dave King, Founding Member, born 1939
Studied: Manchester University
Qualifications: BA Barch RIBA

James Weston, born 1969
Studied: Liverpool School of Architecture and Building Engineering
Qualifications: BA(Hons) First Class, Barch

Projects include
Redevelopment of former Bryant and May match factory 2000
Collegiate School Regeneration 1999
Ricci bar/cafe and retail development 1998
Liverpool Hope University Information Centre, UK 1996

Awards
Modo (part of Concert Square) RIBA award 1997, Civic Trust award 1998
Guild of Students, Liverpool University, British Steel award 1996
School House, Trafford Park Manchester, RIBA award 1996

WESTON WILLIAMSON

70 Cowcross Street
London EC1M 6EJ
Founded 1985

Directors
Andrew Weston, Chris Williamson and Steve Humphreys

Andrew Weston, born 1956
Studied: Leicester School of Architecture
Qualifications: BA(Hons) DipArch(Dist) RIBA CSD Leicester School of Architecture.
Graduated with prizes for dissertation and thesis.

Chris Williamson, born 1956
Studied: Leicester School of Architecture, South Bank Polytechnic and University of Westminster
Qualifications: BA(Hons) DipArch RIBA FRSA MAPM MRTPI

Steve Humphreys, born 1954
Studied: Leicester School of Architecture
Qualifications: BA(Hons) DipArch RIBA

Projects include
East Croydon bus station, 2000
London Bridge Station, 1999
Meyer substation, Royal Albert Dock, London 1999
Excel Energy Centre, Royal Albert Dock, London 1999
National Energy Foundation headquarters, Milton Keynes 1999
St John's Church Hall, Pinner, Middlesex, 1995
Marketplace Design Studios, London 1990
Mexx UK Distribution headquarters, London 1989
Westminster School Science Centre, London 1986
AJ Vines Design Studios, London 1985

Awards
Millennium Projects Award, 1998
Aluminium Imagination Award, 1997
Civic Trust Award, 1996
RIBA Regional Award, 1995
Croydon Urban Design Award, 1989
Meyer International Award, 1987
Glass and Glazing Federation Award, 1985